W9-CKF-669

NEW PENGUIN SHAKESPEARE

GENERAL EDITOR: T. J. B. SPENCER

NS17

WILLIAM SHAKESPEARE

*

THE TWO GENTLEMEN OF VERONA

EDITED BY
NORMAN SANDERS

PENGUIN BOOKS

Penguin Books Ltd, Harmondsworth, Middlesex, England
Penguin Books, 625 Madison Avenue, New York, New York 10022, U.S.A.
Penguin Books Australia Ltd, Ringwood, Victoria, Australia
Penguin Books Canada Ltd, 2801 John Street, Markham, Ontario, Canada L3R 1B4
Penguin Books (N.Z.) Ltd, 182–190 Wairau Road, Auckland 10

—

This edition first published in Penguin Books 1968
Reprinted 1981

—

—

Made and printed in Great Britain
by Richard Clay (The Chaucer Press) Ltd,
Bungay, Suffolk
Set in Monotype Ehrhardt

CONTENTS

INTRODUCTION

DURING the past fifty years or so, either through the efforts of revaluating critics or as a result of imaginative theatrical revival, some of Shakespeare's plays which were held in low esteem during the eighteenth and nineteenth centuries have been shown to possess unsuspected qualities. *The Two Gentlemen of Verona* is almost the sole exception; the few defensive critical reassessments that have been attempted have not won general acceptance, and modern stage productions have mostly failed to discover any of the sparkle or deep seriousness which have been found in plays like *The Comedy of Errors* or *All's Well that Ends Well*. Alone in the canon, it has afforded critics a relief from bardolatry; they have been able to be as severe in their strictures as were their eighteenth-century predecessors.

All are agreed on the play's immaturity; its inclusion in the list of Shakespeare's works published by Francis Meres in his *Palladis Tamia* proves only that it had been written if not performed by 1598, and most scholars would place its composition from four to eight years earlier on the grounds of its style and its relationship to other plays. This means that it belongs in that quartet of early comedies which are often labelled 'experimental'. In each of these plays Shakespeare appears to have been deliberately extending his range by handling very different kinds of comic materials and employing widely varied dramatic techniques. In *The Comedy of Errors* he took as source material two classical Latin plays and fashioned a complex plot with a farcical surface and dark undertones; in *The Taming of the Shrew* he reworked the old shrew-taming legend into a riotous comedy containing implicit comment on the social and marital *mores* of the time; and in *Love's Labour's Lost* he composed a scintillating conversation piece on the favourite Renaissance topic of Nature versus Art, replete with contemporary satire, exquisite and conceited lyric poetry, and type characters like those found in the popular Italian *Commedia dell'Arte*. It is in *The Two Gentlemen of Verona* especially, however, that Shakespeare appears to have turned his attention to the technical problems inherent in the dramatization of materials drawn from the genre known as Romance. These materials were to be the major ingredients of all his mature comedies, and he was to use them in still greater concentration when writing his four final plays.

THE ROMANCE ELEMENTS

The Two Gentlemen of Verona is almost a complete anthology of the practices of the doctrine of romantic love which inspired the poetic and prose Romances of the period. For example, one can find the rhapsody on female beauty and the elevation of the mistress to a more than human plane in Valentine's praise of Silvia (III.1.174–5, 178–81):

> *What light is light, if Silvia be not seen?*
> *What joy is joy, if Silvia be not by? . . .*
> *Except I be by Silvia in the night,*
> *There is no music in the nightingale;*
> *Unless I look on Silvia in the day,*
> *There is no day for me to look upon.*

Along with this there is the inevitable torment of the unrequited lover, showing itself in stereotyped posturing and conventional vocabulary (II.4.127–33):

> *I have done penance for contemning Love,*
> *Whose high imperious thoughts have punished me*
> *With bitter fasts, with penitential groans,*
> *With nightly tears, and daily heart-sore sighs;*
> *For, in revenge of my contempt of love,*
> *Love hath chased sleep from my enthrallèd eyes,*
> *And made them watchers of mine own heart's sorrow.*

Typical also of the Romance world is the subjection of love to strain from both without and within: in Proteus's case by his father's command which separates him from his mistress in the beginning and by his own fickle nature which falls prey to momentary sensual attraction; and in Valentine's case by his own stupidity and the Duke's decree of banishment.

Many lesser Romance features make their appearance too: the change from an urban to a rural environment in the latter part of the play; Valentine's appreciation of the benefits of the natural life as against the corruptions of the city (V.4.2–3):

> *This shadowy desert, unfrequented woods,*
> *I better brook than flourishing peopled towns;*

the disguise, journey, and trials of the deserted heroine as she makes her way to Milan in pursuit of Proteus; the chance meeting and involvement of Valentine with the impossibly unreal outlaws; and, finally, all the trappings of the play – its travels, midnight *rendez-vous*, serenades, forests, rope-ladders, towers, confessors, and love-lorn knight protectors.

However, while Shakespeare uses the conventions of the Romance genre, he also simultaneously provides a comic critique of them – chiefly, though not exclusively, through the two clowns, Speed and Launce. From the first scene of the play it is obviously Speed's dramatic function to supply a mundane view of the idealistic flights of fancy indulged in by Proteus and Valentine. Thus, in his first exchange with Proteus (in I.1), the beloved Julia is seen through his eyes as but another 'mutton', and later he finds his own master, Valentine, an easy subject for his satirical picturing of erotic dejection (II.1.17–30):

> first, you have learned, like Sir Proteus, to wreathe your arms, like a malcontent; to relish a love-song, like a robin-redbreast; to walk alone, like one that had the pestilence; to sigh, like a schoolboy that had lost his ABC; to weep, like a young wench that had buried her grandam; to fast, like one that takes diet; to watch, like one that fears robbing; to speak puling, like a beggar at Hallowmas. You were wont, when you laughed, to crow like a cock; when you walked, to walk like one of the lions; when you fasted, it was presently after dinner; when you looked sadly, it was for want of money. And now you are metamorphosed with a mistress, that, when I look on you, I can hardly think you are my master.

It is Speed who comments on the encounter between Silvia and Valentine as they move through the stilted ritual of a Romance courtship (II.1); and, later still, his conversation with Launce in III.1 provides an indirect commentary on the young gentlemen's love affairs by offering as a contrast Launce's own crude and materialistic peasant *amour*.

Comic qualification of the standards of the Romance code is also found in the detached analyses of the conventions of courtship made by the lovers themselves – for example, Valentine's instructions to the Duke of Milan on how to win a reluctant mistress (III.1.89–130), and Proteus's lesson to Thurio on the arts of midnight wooing (III.2.67–87).

In both his use of and satire upon these Romance materials, Shakespeare was almost certainly influenced by popular contemporary examples in the genre. The scenes that depict the Julia–Proteus courtship early in the play and those that are concerned with her disguise, her witnessing her lover's unfaithfulness, and her serving him as a page were found by Shakespeare either in the original Spanish version of Jorge de Montemayor's story of Felix and Felismena which forms a part of his *La Diana* (published in Valencia in 1542) or in the French or English translations of it. He may well have been familiar also with similar situations in Sir Philip Sidney's *Arcadia* or in a lost play, probably based on Montemayor's story, called *The History of Felix and Philiomena*, recorded in the Revels Accounts as having been acted by the Queen's Men's Company before the Court at Greenwich Palace on 3 January 1595. The blending of the Romance love ethic and the comic burlesque of it was a feature of the plays of John Lyly, which Shakespeare appears to have known well; and many miscellaneous details, like the hero's captaincy of an outlaw band, the midnight meeting, and the rope-ladder device, may well have been adopted from the *Arcadia*, or Arthur Brooke's poem *Romeus and Juliet*, or Anthony Mundy's plays on Robert Earl of Huntingdon.

Of at least equal importance in the play with the theme of love is that of the conflicting demands of friendship and sexual attraction. It was from classical literature that the Renaissance ultimately derived its ideal of friendship between men, even as its medieval heritage was the source for the Renaissance stress on the importance of heterosexual love. By the time Shakespeare was writing *The Two*

Gentlemen of Verona, a large body of literature had been composed on the theme of the conflicting claims of these two values – including the most popular novel of the period, John Lyly's *Euphues, The Anatomy of Wit*, as well as some of his plays. However, it has been convincingly argued that Shakespeare was probably most influenced in his treatment of this theme by Sir Thomas Elyot's *The Book of the Governor* (1531); in Book II, Chapter 12 of this is related the story of Titus and Gisippus – a tale which bears certain close resemblances to the Valentine–Proteus–Silvia plot, of which the most important is that, at the story's end, Gisippus, like Valentine, offers his mistress to his friend.

PROBLEMS AND WEAKNESSES

In *The Two Gentlemen of Verona* Shakespeare clearly faced certain problems in attempting to give dramatic form to the materials of a literary genre that depended for its effects on narrative spread, spatial range, a great variety of situations, largely incredible character motivation, and unspecific geographical location. And, as has often been pointed out, there are abundant signs in the play of the strain that these problems imposed.

To begin with, the play's geography is both inaccurate and inconsistent. Proteus and Valentine go from Verona to Milan by sea, whereas it is clear that the disguised Julia intends to make the journey between the two cities by land, as does Valentine returning after his banishment. The Duke of Milan in III.1.81 appears to imagine that the dukedom he rules is Verona rather than Milan; and (II.5.1) Speed, in Milan, welcomes his friend Launce to Padua (see Commentary).

Next, Shakespeare was unable to maintain in his dramatic treatment the necessary balance between the

Romance convention within which he was working and the kind of characterization demanded by this convention. Valentine is obviously intended to be the focus of romantic sympathy as an attractive, idealistic young man whose love for Silvia is credible and whose youthful responses, first to Proteus's love affair and later to his own difficulties, are the result of an accurate if not very profound observation of human nature. Yet he is manipulated like a puppet by the Duke, and is presented as the risible object of the wit of both Speed and Silvia. To a lesser degree the character of Proteus suffers also, for the interest generated by his reactions to his moral dilemma is disproportionate to the stereotyped role he has to enact as a false friend and treacherous lover. Julia, too, at one moment in the play (V.2), comments on Thurio's pretensions as a suitor in a Speed-like manner that is out of keeping with her character as it has been depicted up to this point. Among the other figures, Silvia apparently loses both tongue and intelligence in the final scene, and her would-be protector and champion, Sir Eglamour, is set up as the ideal courtly lover and chivalric knight in one scene (IV.3) only to be knocked down as a coward at his first testing (V.3).

Perhaps the best illustration, however, of the playwright being led by his dramatic instincts and his interest in human nature to overload his conventional framework occurs in the final scene. There, in accordance with the precedents in the so-called 'brotherhood' stories, Shakespeare insists on presenting the ultimate trial of the true friend and has Valentine restore Proteus to his favour and then offer him his own mistress. Probably the Elizabethan audience would have had less difficulty in accepting this action than we do in the twentieth century. Nevertheless, the different mode in which Shakespeare seems to have been working in the creation of character in other parts of the play prevents our easy acceptance at this point of the sudden demand that we regard the actors as merely Romance stereotypes.

Weaknesses of other kinds and of a more technical nature have also been charged against the play. Even at a first reading, the uneven quality of the verse is striking, with some exquisite lyric utterance jostled by blank verse lines of a remorselessly pedestrian kind. More fundamentally, one critic has convincingly demonstrated the limited dramatic technique, noting the use of only three devices (the soliloquy, the duologue, and the aside as comment) in some thirteen of the twenty scenes. One result of this is that when the dialogue involves three or more persons, some characters are left unaccountably silent on the stage. For example, Speed remains mute during a great part of II.4 (see Commentary II.4.7); Thurio stands tongue-tied for about fifty lines in the same scene, and makes an entrance in III.1 only to be dismissed after one line; and in the outlaw scenes the lack of conversational cohesion among the characters is painfully obvious.

Nevertheless, despite all the acknowledged weaknesses of the play most students of Shakespeare would underwrite Dr Johnson's over-all impression: 'When I read this play I cannot but think that I discover both in the serious and ludicrous scenes, the language and sentiments of Shakespeare.' Many of the playwright's favourite character-types, themes, situations, and details make their first appearance in this play in a recognizably Shakespearian form. Valentine is the dramatic ancestor of those other love-stricken young men, Bassanio, Orlando, Orsino, and, particularly, the tragic Romeo. Julia is an early version of Rosalind, in following her lover from the court to the forest; of Viola, in entering the service of her lover–master and promoting his suit to another lady; and of Portia, in her witty discussion with her maid of her suitors' strengths and weaknesses. Silvia, like the later Imogen, is offered a quite perfect serenade by an unwelcome suitor. And there are a host of smaller anticipatory details: Valentine laments his banishment in almost the same words as Romeo, and, like Romeo, he employs a rope-ladder; Launce anticipates the idiom of the Young Gobbo and Bottom the Weaver; Valentine finds a philosophy in his forced retreat into the woods similar to the banished Duke's in *As You Like It*; and Proteus has the same difficulty in distinguishing between appearances and reality as does the Claudio of *Much Ado About Nothing*.

THEMES AND TECHNIQUES IN THE LOVE PLOT

The Two Gentlemen of Verona, however, throws far more light on Shakespeare's later comic vision than any listing of dramatic situations and character-types would suggest. Simply because the play reveals a relatively unsure dramatist at work and many effects managed with a tiro's lack of expertise, it offers us an opportunity to see more clearly than anywhere else in the canon what were to become characteristic techniques. It stands as an 'anatomie' or show-through version, as it were, of Shakespeare's comic art and helps us to understand in part the least appreciated section of the poet's work.

It is obvious from the deployment of the two pairs of lovers that Shakespeare was aiming at a dramatic contrast between two divergent attitudes to love, embodied in Valentine and Proteus respectively; and, further, that Julia was to represent some special standard of constancy and ultimate test of love's reality, taking up a position between the two heroes. In a manner that was to become typical, this contrast was to be reinforced on the narrative level by the balancing of character against character and situation against situation. On the poetic plane, echoing words and iterative imagery were clearly designed to interrelate and develop key ideas or attitudes associated with the different aspects of love presented.

So far as the poetic effects are concerned, it is the verbal implications of the love-at-first-sight convention that provide the leading images. Proteus is invariably associated, both in his honest and dishonourable love affairs, with that kind of affection which resides in the eyes rather than the mind. In the first scene of the play, Valentine starts the pattern of imagery when he says (I.1.3-4) he would desire Proteus's company on his travels

> Were't not affection chains thy tender days
> To the sweet glances of thy honoured love,

and Proteus himself maintains the same note, ironically in view of subsequent events, when he asks his friend (lines 12-13) to

> Think on thy Proteus, when thou haply seest
> Some rare noteworthy object in thy travel.

Then, as the scene ends, we find him fearing the existence of a similar tendency in Julia in matters of appearance and value (lines 149-50):

> I fear my Julia would not deign my lines,
> Receiving them from such a worthless post.

Having thus verbally established Proteus's standard of affection, Shakespeare provides one element of contrast by dramatic rather than poetic means in an incident which relates to the lines quoted above. In the scene immediately following, we are introduced to the object of Proteus's devotion, Julia. In her exchange with her maid, Lucetta, she actively rejects the value of shallow, eye-residing affection in refusing to look at Proteus's written protestations and destroying the letter while her maid is present. At the same time, she leaves us in no doubt as to the strength of her love; her desire is to have the letter forced to her view because she would she 'knew [Proteus's] mind'. Placing less emphasis than her lover on the appearance of things, she knows she can teach her 'brow to frown', even though an 'inward joy' compels her 'heart to smile'. Julia knows, in short, as does the later Helena of *A Midsummer Night's Dream*, that 'Love looks not with the eyes, but with the mind'. However, unfortunately for her, Proteus, unlike Demetrius in the wood near Athens, will find in Milan neither an omnipresent Puck nor a curative herb.

Even in those passages of poetry where Proteus's expression of his passion carries lyrical conviction, we find him couching his declaration both negatively and in terms of a natural changeability (I.3.84–7):

> *O, how this spring of love resembleth*
> *The uncertain glory of an April day,*
> *Which now shows all the beauty of the sun,*
> *And by and by a cloud takes all away.*

It is, however, on the narrative level that Proteus's standards of value are tested: in his meeting with Valentine and Silvia after he arrives in Milan (like the later Claudio of *Much Ado About Nothing*) his visually orientated affection is unable to withstand even a first trial. The highly conceited and neo-Petrarchan exchanges between Silvia and Valentine in the second act of the play (II.4.85–92) maintain the pattern of visual images of the earlier scenes:

VALENTINE
This is the gentleman I told your ladyship

Had come along with me but that his mistress
Did hold his eyes locked in her crystal looks.

SILVIA

Belike that now she hath enfranchised them
Upon some other pawn for fealty.

VALENTINE

Nay, sure, I think she holds them prisoners still.

SILVIA

Nay, then, he should be blind; and, being blind,
How could he see his way to seek out you?

In the later conversation between the two friends, after
Silvia has left the stage, their contrasting attitudes to love
are projected by a formalized parallelism of phrase.
Proteus describes Silvia as an idol to be worshipped,
against which Valentine names her a heavenly saint; and
to the latter's claim for her divinity, Proteus admits only
that she is an earthly paragon. Even allowing for the
conventional exaggeration of style in this passage, Shakespeare is clearly showing us one man reaching for a semi-
spiritual, Petrarchan definition of his affection while the
other is more than content with the earthly limitations of
the lady he has but had 'a look of'. After Valentine's exit,
these various allusions are drawn together in Proteus's
soliloquy, extending the impression thus far created by the
introduction of new though related metaphors. Silvia is
a 'newer object' which causes the remembrance of his
former love to be quite forgotten; her perfections so blind
him that his love for his previous mistress is like a waxen
image which, when exposed to heat, will lose the 'impression of the thing it' is. It is interesting that when Julia
later makes use of a similar figure of speech, it is to convey
the all-consuming irresistible power of faithful love whose
'extreme rage' can be neither qualified nor dammed up.

On the other hand, Shakespeare's management of the second element in his opposition of the contrasting types of love is much less sure. Clearly he intended to set against this all too visually receptive Proteus a Valentine who is intellectually blinkered but emotionally clear-sighted. In Valentine's soliloquy after he has been banished by the Duke for aspiring to Silvia's hand, the verbal associations convey an attitude to love in sharp contrast with that of Proteus (III.1.174–7, 182–4):

> *What light is light, if Silvia be not seen?*
> *What joy is joy, if Silvia be not by?*
> *Unless it be to think that she is by,*
> *And feed upon the shadow of perfection. . . .*
> *She is my essence, and I leave to be,*
> *If I be not by her fair influence*
> *Fostered, illumined, cherished, kept alive.*

Here, unlike Proteus, he asserts the value of the substance rather than the shadow, of the tangible reality rather than the appearance; for him, love demands the surrender of self in order to create another 'essence' without which he will 'leave to be', and for which there can be no substitute. In this he is the first of the line of Shakespearian lovers who see truly both the inward as well as the outward beauty of their mistresses.

However, while Shakespeare's intention is clearly to counterbalance the two young men and their ways of seeing and loving, its execution is less happy. Whereas Proteus becomes more interesting as he moves from love of Julia, through a half-regretted fascination with outward show, on to a fond idolatry and violent lust, before making a sudden volte-face in the final scene, Valentine vacillates between lyric utterance and colourless mediocrity, before exhibiting what is perhaps fatal to the romantic hero –

namely, sheer stupidity. First, we witness him blundering through the letter scene with Silvia (II.1), where he is unable to perceive the rather graceful courtly gesture by which his mistress declares her love for him, even though, as Speed's commentary on the device assures us (lines 128–9), it is a

> *jest unseen, inscrutable, invisible*
> *As a nose on a man's face, or a weathercock on a steeple!*

Later, in III.1, he stands chatting with Silvia's father, with his rope-ladder under his cloak, and is tricked into making known the plans for his projected elopement by means of a ludicrously obvious stratagem on the Duke's part. Next, he is brought into contact with the impossible outlaws, whom one critic has appositely compared to the Pirates of Penzance, and who elect him their captain on the strength of his good looks and his skill in speaking foreign languages. Finally, his adherence to the friendship code obliges him to surrender his mistress to his newly-repentant friend with one of the most impossible lines in the English dramatic repertory (V.4.83). Shakespeare was, of course, to make his audience accept greater incongruities than these later in his career; but here the character of Valentine as created is unable to withstand the strain of incredibility to which these encounters subject it. The result is a hiatus in the dramatic design as Valentine fails to offer any truly effective counterbalance to the figure of Proteus.

In view of this character weakness, one has some sympathy with those critics who have insisted that there is a good deal more allegory in the creation of Valentine than has generally been admitted. In his adventures there has been discerned a pattern similar to that found in the medieval poem and handbook of the Courtly Love code, the *Roman de la Rose*, and Valentine may be seen to pass through the same stages as the Courtly Lover, and to be tested with the same object – that of conquering self and emerging from the shadows into the reality postulated in Platonic theory. Nevertheless, it has to be admitted that, even with this allegorical content, in theatrical terms the character lacks the necessary dramatic interest to share with Proteus the audience's empathetic involvement. For, while Proteus too is in general a flat creation, there are moments in the play at which he enlists our interest, if not our sympathy. For example, his soliloquy in II.4 at least raises a problem of moral choice and conveys a degree of uncertainty which generates curiosity in the audience (lines 211–12):

> *If I can check my erring love, I will;*
> *If not, to compass her I'll use my skill.*

His later soliloquy develops this interest and there is a degree of psychological credibility as Proteus poses his dilemma (II.6.1–8):

> *To leave my Julia, shall I be forsworn;*
> *To love fair Silvia, shall I be forsworn;*
> *To wrong my friend, I shall be much forsworn.*
> *And e'en that power which gave me first my oath*
> *Provokes me to this threefold perjury:*
> *Love bade me swear, and Love bids me forswear.*
> *O sweet-suggesting Love, if thou hast sinned,*
> *Teach me, thy tempted subject, to excuse it!*

We feel some personal involvement, of a kind unprovoked by any other character in the play save Julia, as he draws together the excuses for his infidelity: the superior beauty of Silvia (lines 9–10):

> *At first I did adore a twinkling star,*
> *But now I worship a celestial sun;*

the plea that he is a victim of an emotion which threatens his very identity – his mistaken 'essence' (lines 19–22):

> *Julia I lose, and Valentine I lose;*
> *If I keep them, I needs must lose myself;*
> *If I lose them, thus find I by their loss:*
> *For Valentine, myself; for Julia, Silvia;*

and the elevation of a false conception of love so that it appears to conform to legitimate romantic aspiration (line 24): 'For love is still most precious in itself'. His final decision in favour of active villainy is also made credible to us by the lines incongruously linking his now debased conception of love with his betrayal of friendship (lines 42–3):

> *Love, lend me wings to make my purpose swift,*
> *As thou hast lent me wit to plot this drift.*

Certainly there is no great subtlety here, but there is a psychological dimension which is totally absent so far as Valentine is concerned; and at certain points later in the play, odd lines carry a conviction of his humanity, as when (IV.2.12–15) he laments Silvia's

> *sudden quips,*
> *The least whereof would quell a lover's hope,*
> *Yet, spaniel-like, the more she spurns my love*
> *The more it grows and fawneth on her still.*

Interest in Proteus as a dramatic creation is strengthened by his close relationship with Julia and particularly by the role she plays in the later portions of the play. She is much more realistically conceived than either of the two leading male characters. Through a mixture of comic observation and the projection of human inconsistency and genuine feeling, Julia is believably portrayed in the letter scene

(I.2), and emerges as the first of those comic heroines of Shakespeare who are idealized by their lovers, but who impress the audience by their combination of practical good sense and healthy sensuality. It is true that Julia has all the romantic convictions of a young woman in love, and can lyrically transform her projected disguise and journey as a page to Milan into an odyssey of true love (II.7.24–38):

> The more thou dammest it up, the more it burns.
> The current that with gentle murmur glides,
> Thou knowest, being stopped, impatiently doth rage;
> But when his fair course is not hinderèd,
> He makes sweet music with th'enamelled stones,
> Giving a gentle kiss to every sedge
> He overtaketh in his pilgrimage;
> And so by many winding nooks he strays,
> With willing sport, to the wild ocean.
> Then let me go, and hinder not my course.
> I'll be as patient as a gentle stream,
> And make a pastime of each weary step,
> Till the last step have brought me to my love;
> And there I'll rest as, after much turmoil,
> A blessèd soul doth in Elysium.

But she can also place the pieces of Proteus's love letter in her bosom in warm contrition, with the words (I.2.128–9):

> Thus will I fold them one upon another.
> Now kiss, embrace, contend, do what you will.

It is, however, during the later parts of the play that Julia acts out her most important role in connexion with the conflict of values represented by Proteus and Valentine. Just before the Duke's banishment of Valentine, it is clear that, by the logical development of the metaphor of sight which has been associated with him, Proteus's attraction to

Silvia is no longer merely visual but has become icono-latric. He sees her as an object rather than as a person, as his description of her pleading before her father suggests (III.1.224–31):

> *A sea of melting pearl, which some call tears;*
> *Those at her father's churlish feet she tendered;*
> *With them, upon her knees, her humble self,*
> *Wringing her hands, whose whiteness so became them*
> *As if but now they waxèd pale for woe.*
> *But neither bended knees, pure hands held up,*
> *Sad sighs, deep groans, nor silver-shedding tears,*
> *Could penetrate her uncompassionate sire.*

The poetic focus here is pictorial rather than emotional, as Proteus views the scene almost exclusively in terms of attitude, grouping, and colour. That pearls should be seen as tears is an unnatural inversion of a metaphor, which effectively deprives the act of weeping of its passionate origin; and the stress laid on the bending of the knee, the whiteness of the hands, and their static pose of supplica-tion, ignores the feeling animating the attitude. Even when emotion is introduced, it is negatively conveyed in the father's rage rather than in the daughter's sorrow. In fact, in these lines Silvia ceases to be herself and becomes simply the image of a girl pleading with a father.

It is easy to see, in view of this development, what Shakespeare was attempting to do in the episodes leading to the gift of Silvia's portrait in the fourth act. Having been refused possession of Silvia's person, Proteus character-istically settles for ownership of a picture of her. Whereas Valentine in his soliloquy (quoted on page 19 above) refused to feed upon the 'shadow of perfection' when the substance was not by, this is precisely what Proteus begs to be allowed to do (IV.2.116–22):

Madam, if your heart be so obdurate,
Vouchsafe me yet your picture for my love,
The picture that is hanging in your chamber;
To that I'll speak, to that I'll sigh and weep,
For since the substance of your perfect self
Is else devoted, I am but a shadow;
And to your shadow will I make true love.

To this relatively simple dramatic connexion between
Proteus's standard of values and consequent action,
Shakespeare adds an extra dimension by having Proteus
employ the disguised Julia as the agent by which Silvia's
portrait is brought to him. In one sense her page's costume
makes Julia physically what Proteus is both nominally and
morally: that is, a shape-changer, a metamorphosis.
However, in her case, the transformation is a proof of
constancy of affection rather than of emotional fickleness.
As she notes herself (V.4.109–10):

It is the lesser blot, modesty finds,
Women to change their shapes than men their minds.

The theme of the shadow–reality dichotomy is still
further developed in Julia's meeting with Silvia, although
there is no real opposition in the scene because both women
are in agreement about Proteus's behaviour and the value
of true and faithful love. Thus the exchange between them
is pathetic, decorative, and conceited rather than dramatically exciting. Nevertheless, the form which the decoration
and conceit takes is interesting in so far as it shows an
attempt to develop the ideas of 'shadow' and 'shape-
changing' through dramatic rather than poetic metaphor.
In reply to Silvia's question about the height of Proteus's
previous mistress, Julia replies (IV.4.155–69):

> *About my stature; for, at Pentecost,*
> *When all our pageants of delight were played,*
> *Our youth got me to play the woman's part*
> *And I was trimmed in Madam Julia's gown,*
> *Which servèd me as fit, by all men's judgements,*
> *As if the garment had been made for me;*
> *Therefore I know she is about my height.*
> *And at that time I made her weep agood,*
> *For I did play a lamentable part.*
> *Madam, 'twas Ariadne passioning*
> *For Theseus' perjury and unjust flight;*
> *Which I so lively acted with my tears*
> *That my poor mistress, movèd therewithal,*
> *Wept bitterly; and would I might be dead*
> *If I in thought felt not her very sorrow.*

Here we are called upon to peer through a series of shifting illusions, both invented and actual: the real Julia, the role of the page Sebastian that she is playing now, the imaginary role of Ariadne played at the Pentecost revels. But in doing so we discern that it is the imaginary tears elicited from Julia by the supposed performance that represent the emotional reality of her present situation as she stands before the woman with whom Proteus is infatuated.

Just prior to Silvia's entry in IV.4, Julia, like Proteus at his moment of moral choice, considers the significance of her actions and to what extent they constitute a threat to the integrity of her identity; but, unlike him, she decides to deny the claims of immediate self-interest so that she may remain a true servant to her false master. In doing so, of course, she places herself, in terms of the love ethic informing the play, in the same camp as Valentine and Silvia (IV.4.100–104):

> *I am my master's true confirmèd love,*

But cannot be true servant to my master,
Unless I prove false traitor to myself.
Yet will I woo for him, but yet so coldly
As, heaven it knows, I would not have him speed.

As she delivers her portrait to Julia, it is Silvia who underlines the spiritually misshapen quality of Proteus's fickleness, and, a few lines later, it is ironical that she performs without any inner reservations the same action as Julia has in I.2 in tearing up Proteus's letter (IV.4.115–17, 125–8):

Go, give your master this. Tell him from me,
One Julia, that his changing thoughts forget,
Would better fit his chamber than this shadow. . . .
I will not look upon your master's lines.
I know they are stuffed with protestations,
And full of new-found oaths, which he will break
As easily as I do tear his paper.

However, later, it is Julia who, in a second soliloquy, with Silvia's portrait in her hands, makes clear the point that Shakespeare has been developing about the true lover's imagination, and adds yet another touch of femininity which rounds out Julia's character still further (IV.4.191–202):

What should it be that he respects in her
But I can make respective in myself,
If this fond Love were not a blinded god?
Come, shadow, come, and take this shadow up,
For 'tis thy rival. O, thou senseless form,
Thou shalt be worshipped, kissed, loved, and adored!
And were there sense in his idolatry,
My substance should be statue in thy stead.
I'll use thee kindly for thy mistress' sake,

> *That used me so ; or else, by Jove I vow,*
> *I should have scratched out your unseeing eyes,*
> *To make my master out of love with thee!*

It is in the articulation of what might be called 'the picture theme' that one may find a possible explanation of the most notorious textual crux in the play. At the end of II.4, during which Proteus has talked with Silvia and Valentine for a space of some eighty lines or so, Proteus assures himself in soliloquy that he has unaccountably begun to love Silvia although, as he says (II.4.207–10):

> *'Tis but her picture I have yet beheld,*
> *And that hath dazzlèd my reason's light ;*
> *But when I look on her perfections,*
> *There is no reason but I shall be blind.*

If, as it would appear, Shakespeare designed to have the picture scene closely integrated with the themes of moral change and the deluding imagination associated with the lover, then it seems likely that Silvia's portrait would have made its appearance earlier in the play, possibly during a first meeting of Proteus and Valentine early in the second act, a scene, perhaps, of which the soliloquy at II.4.190–212 might be all that remains.

THE COMIC ELEMENTS

It was a favourite technique of Shakespeare to have his low comic characters both verbally and conceptually related to the more serious elements in his plays. For example, the mechanicals in *A Midsummer Night's Dream*, Dogberry and the watchmen in *Much Ado About Nothing*, and Malvolio, Sir Toby Belch, and Sir Andrew Aguecheek in *Twelfth Night* are all integrated with the central love plots of their various plays on many different levels and by a multiplicity of poetic and dramatic devices. In fact, when one recalls just how much these character groups are an integral part of the plays in which they appear, and further remembers that a development of this technique of inter-relation led ultimately to Prince Hal and Falstaff, then it would perhaps be more accurate to regard it as an essential part of Shakespeare's vision of life as a whole.

In the low comic portions of *The Two Gentlemen of Verona* there is evidence of a similar care and thematic relevance. The two clownish servants, Launce and Speed, are both satirical commentators on their masters' actions and attitudes, particularly where their conventional love posturings are concerned. However, once this common function has been admitted, it is equally clear that their roles are different both in kind and in means of execution.

Speed is the verbal, witty type of clown. He belongs with those clever, prattling schoolboys who inhabit the plays of John Lyly, and with Don Armado's page, Moth, in *Love's Labour's Lost*. His is a brand of cleverness that Shakespeare quickly tired of; he came to prefer more human – and more easily tolerated – clowns, like Touch-stone or Feste on a conscious level, or like Dogberry or Bottom on an unconscious one. Perhaps also this kind of comedy reminded Shakespeare, the adult actor and manager, too forcibly for him to look on it long with favour, of the popular rival Children's Companies, who are called in *Hamlet* those 'little eyases' crying out against their own succession.

But however this may be, Speed is of this kind. He is conscious of every verbal effect he aims at; every quibble he utters is a calculation; he is overtly satirical; and the deviousness of his puns is unmatched elsewhere in Shake-speare. The humour he provides is that of the patter comedian rather than the true clown, and is a product of the incongruity between his comments and the actual situation on which he is commenting. This being so, his relationship to the themes of love, friendship, and human intercourse generally is tenuous at best. He is a burlesque version of neither lover nor friend, save perhaps momentarily when he explains to Valentine that he is in love with his bed rather than a mistress, or when he urges his master to dinner with the observation that 'though the chameleon Love can feed on the air, I am one that am nourished by my victuals, and would fain have meat' (II.1.163–5). More often, his attack is satirically direct, as he criticizes the stupidities of love; it is the clear-eyed view of the emotionally uninvolved which enables him to see through Silvia's courtly device as she tenders Valentine his own letter, while the lover himself stands dulled by love's melancholy. For the rest, however, Speed's role in the play is either purely functional or simply verbally entertaining.

Launce, on the other hand, while certainly able to 'mistake the word' as complicatedly as Speed, is not limited in the same way either in his comic effects or in his dramatic relevance. Instead of just making comedy out of an already existing situation, he can create a comic situation out of a deadly serious response to the events of his life. While Speed observes incidents, Launce, out of himself and in his own terms, creates for the audience his ludicrous family leave-taking or the moment of his dog's disgrace, thus making his involvement total and his three monologues (in II.3, III.1, and IV.4) truly comic. It is thus the parallelism and situational inversion of the scenes with Launce and Crab, rather than the straightforward verbal corrective of those involving Speed, which provide the critically humorous dimension of Proteus's fickleness, Julia's faithfulness, and the Romance code of friendship professed by the two men.

Launce makes his first appearance in the second act, and his monologue describing his parting from his family is clearly a parody of the affectionate leave-taking between Proteus and Julia which immediately precedes it on the stage. The relationships between the two situations are numerous and obviously intended. On the one hand, we witness the silent Julia whom Proteus rebukes for weeping and who leaves without a word; and, on the other hand, the clown depicts mock-epically the laments of his father, mother, and sister, and the heartlessness of his recalcitrant cur, who 'all this while sheds not a tear'. In ironic contrast also are the talkative and soon-to-be-false Proteus who defines the wordlessness of true affection, and the loquacious and sincere Launce who describes the heartless silence of his dog. Verbally, too, echoes abound; for example, Proteus's lines (II.2.13–15):

> *My father stays my coming. Answer not.*
> *The tide is now – nay, not thy tide of tears;*
> *That tide will stay me longer than I should*

are followed by Launce's quibbling with Panthino (II.3.31–42, 48–51):

PANTHINO *Launce, away, away! Aboard! Thy master is shipped, and thou art to post after with oars. What's the matter? Why weepest thou, man? Away, ass, you'll lose the tide, if you tarry any longer.*

LAUNCE *It is no matter if the tied were lost, for it is the unkindest tied that ever any man tied.*

PANTHINO *What's the unkindest tide?*

LAUNCE *Why, he that's tied here, Crab, my dog.*

PANTHINO *Tut, man, I mean thou'lt lose the flood; and, in losing the flood, lose thy voyage; and, in losing thy voyage, lose thy master; and, in losing thy master, lose thy service. . . .*

LAUNCE *Lose the tide, and the voyage, and the master, and
the service, and the tied. Why, man, if the river were dry, I
am able to fill it with my tears. If the wind were down, I
could drive the boat with my sighs.*

Similarly, the meeting of the two servants in Milan in
II.5 immediately succeeds that of their masters, and their
conversation constitutes a commentary on the love theme.
Launce's extreme caution about his own master's love
affair, as he assures Speed 'Thou shalt never get such a
secret from me but by a parable', is an implicit reflection
on Valentine's freely given confidences about Silvia and
himself which puts him in Proteus's power and ultimately
brings about his banishment.

The dramatic parallel thus early set up between the
comic scenes and the love scenes is further developed in
two more episodes. The dialogue in III.1, in which Launce
and Speed read the inventory of the vices and virtues of the
former's *inamorata*, echoes both the friendship and the
love themes. First, it evokes a contrast with the two earlier
letter scenes involving Proteus and Valentine. Secondly, it
offers a world far removed from that of romantic idealiza-
tion: whereas Proteus and Valentine are concerned with
the canons of true love and the concept of spiritual oneness
with the beloved, Launce is preoccupied with marriage
as an economic bargain. In his consideration, halitosis,
toothlessness, and a demonstrable lecherous nature are of
more immediate concern than sparkling eyes which are
Cupid's weapons or the feminine graces that are lent by
heaven. And it is wealth which overcomes all these
deformities for Launce, even as it does for the Duke when
he proposes Thurio for his son-in-law. As the scene ends,
we realize that, like Valentine with Proteus, Launce has
discussed his affair in friendship with Speed; and, as in the

main plot Proteus will be punished for his perfidy, so here Speed will be 'swinged' for reading Launce's paper and be corrected like the 'unmannerly slave' he is for thrusting himself into secrets.

In Launce's final monologue in IV.4, the parallel between master–man and dog–servant on the one hand, and mistress–page and servant–master on the other is developed. The dog Crab is again in disgrace as it enters with Launce, having urinated in Silvia's presence; for this the clown himself has taken the blame and been soundly beaten. In the comic terminology employed, Làunce, the master, has been made the whipping-boy for his dog, the servant. He addresses the audience thus (IV.4.1–15):

When a man's servant shall play the cur with him, look you, it goes hard – one that I brought up of a puppy; one that I saved from drowning, when three or four of his blind brothers and sisters went to it. I have taught him, even as one would say precisely, 'Thus I would teach a dog.' I was sent to deliver him as a present to Mistress Silvia from my master; and I came no sooner into the dining-chamber, but he steps me to her trencher and steals her capon's leg. O, 'tis a foul thing when a cur cannot keep himself in all companies! I would have, as one should say, one that takes upon him to be a dog indeed, to be, as it were, a dog at all things. If I had not had more wit than he, to take a fault upon me that he did, I think verily he had been hanged for't; sure as I live, he had suffered for't.

As the monologue ends, Proteus enters with the disguised Julia and here again we find a reversal of roles. Proteus, the former lover or 'servant' (to use the Courtly Love terminology employed by the lovers themselves), hires Julia, the former 'mistress', as a servant to fetch and carry for him in an affair which is, according to the play's love ethic, perverted. Launce's sacrifice on behalf of his dog is paralleled by Julia's loyalty, and Proteus's treachery by the behaviour of a wretched mongrel who pesters Silvia with his unwelcome attentions. The man who has betrayed his standards of love and friendship is thus equated dramatically with a dog who is 'a very cur'. And, in case we miss the point, Shakespeare has Launce's question 'How many masters would do this for his servant?' echoed by Julia's line 'How many women would do such a message?'

THE NATURE OF THE COMIC ACHIEVEMENT

It can therefore be argued that the comic scenes do not simply satirize and belittle the love and friendship codes subscribed to in the main plot, but reveal them in a new light. These scenes are the method whereby the characters in the central love situation are shown in terms of a reality which exists even though they ignore it. It is by such methods that Shakespeare makes real and recognizable his Romance world, and, indeed, relates his comic world itself to the actual world of which it is a part.

One scene in the play is particularly successful in performing this essentially Shakespearian feat. It is when the disguised Julia arrives in Milan: she is led by the Host of the Inn to where she may watch her lover as he serenades Silvia under the guise of aiding Thurio's courtship. The song itself is an early example of Shakespeare's lyric skill – a skill later to be exercised extensively in *A Midsummer Night's Dream*, as well as in the other mature comedies. As such its verbal beauty as well as its Petrarchan spiritual values is at odds with both the standards of the singer, Proteus, and the fatuity of Thurio on whose behalf the performance is nominally taking place. This is the first though not the last occasion on which Shakespeare was to link a beautiful song with an unworthy performer; for example, the vicious and foolish Cloten in *Cymbeline* is provided with an equally fine song, 'Hark, hark! The lark at heaven's gate sings', for his adulterous serenading of Imogen. The song in *The Two Gentlemen of Verona* emphasizes musically the distance between Proteus's protestations and the reality of his fickle nature. However, and more important, it is also the means whereby Julia learns of her lover's faithlessness, and by which Shakespeare deepens and widens the issues raised by the central love theme of the play. As the Host and Julia stand watching the musical performance and while the instrumental postlude is being played, they comment in aside to the audience in this way (IV.2.53–69):

HOST *How now? Are you sadder than you were before?*
  How do you, man? The music likes you not.
JULIA *You mistake; the musician likes me not.*
HOST *Why, my pretty youth?*
JULIA *He plays false, father.*
HOST *How? Out of tune on the strings?*
JULIA *Not so; but yet so false that he grieves my very heart-*
  strings.
HOST *You have a quick ear.*
JULIA *Ay, I would I were deaf; it makes me have a slow*
  heart.
HOST *I perceive you delight not in music.*
JULIA *Not a whit, when it jars so.*
HOST *Hark, what fine change is in the music!*
JULIA *Ay; that change is the spite.*
HOST *You would have them always play but one thing?*
JULIA
  I would always have one play but one thing.

This exchange contains a fusion of the verbal and the situational which suggests by means of a series of quibbles a contact between what we are watching on the stage and some wider perspective. It is one of the earliest occasions in Shakespeare where a specific personal issue is linked allusively to the universal. In this case, the troubles of a particular love affair are seen to be at odds with the principle of earthly harmony which, to the Elizabethans, was easily visualized as a reflection of that greater divine harmony, known as, and symbolized by, the music of the spheres. As such, this exchange is a simple example of the same magic by which Macbeth's deed of murder is shown as infecting Scotland and the very well-springs of life itself, and by which Goneril's and Regan's inhumanity to King Lear both reflects and becomes Nature's own indifference to suffering mankind.

As this short scene plays itself out, the Host and Julia are the last remaining characters on the stage. Julia turns to her companion and with a heavy heart says, 'Host, will you go?' to which he replies, rousing himself, 'By my halidom, I was fast asleep.' This two-line exchange contains within it one important aspect of the whole spirit of Shakespeare's comic vision. For here is suggested fleetingly what was to be conveyed much more complexly and centrally in the later plays: namely, a human viewpoint other than that which is at the focus of the play's action. At this point, the audience is reminded that while to Julia the music can have one set of implications – that is, the infidelity of her lover and the disharmony possible in the human heart – to the Host it is simply a concord of sweet sounds. Similarly, even as the overheard Proteus–Silvia dialogue is personally central to Julia's life and dramatically central to the audience's theatrical concern, so to the Host it has been merely a sleep-inducing episode. This is

the kind of effect that Dr Johnson was seeking to define
when he spoke of Shakespeare's plays as

> *exhibiting the real state of sublunary nature, which
> partakes of good and evil, joy and sorrow, mingled with
> endless variety of proportion and innumerable modes of
> combination . . . in which, at the same time, the reveller is
> hasting to his wine, and the mourner burying his friend.*
> Preface to his edition of Shakespeare, 1765

In all his comedies, Shakespeare conveys this dual
vision, and reveals his awareness of two standards of
reality: that of the audience and that of the play. Re-
peatedly, he stresses the one or the other, and, by oscillat-
ing between them, effectively destroys the audience–actor
division. By a variety of devices – songs, asides, solilo-
quies, direct address – characters like Puck, Benedick,
Feste, Bottom, and Rosalind cross the stage front, as it
were, and join the audience's world. Conversely, by
techniques like the overhearing trick, parallel sympathy, or
reflective dramatic situations, the audience is drawn into
the world of the play. With the fundamental division in
the theatre, represented by the stage-front, thus broken or
at least blurred, Shakespeare is able to create a new reality
which includes and transcends the other two. Two
observations of interest may be made perhaps about this
reality. First, it provides both the audience and the play
with the opportunity of being both committed and
detached, of possessing longsight and nearsight, of belong-
ing and witnessing. Second, it is the result, not so much of
the fact that Shakespeare draws some of the materials of
his comic art from the theatre or merely makes use of a
knowledge of the theatrical experience, as of the fact that
his vision's very being is located in the stage world.
Shakespeare's comedies are truly theatre as well as drama.

However, it is only in comic masterpieces like *Twelfth Night* or *As You Like It* that we find this vision perfectly and completely articulated and embodied. In *The Two Gentlemen of Verona* it can be detected only from time to time. Yet, the fact that it does appear in scenes like the one discussed above or in the relationship that some of the comic scenes have to the main plot is one reason for the failure of the play as a whole. These small triumphs prevent the audience accepting those longer sections of the play in which Shakespeare falls back into the stilted characteristics and idiom of the Romance convention.

Nowhere in the piece is this more obvious than in the much-criticized final scene. From the text as we have it in the Folio of 1623, Shakespeare appears to be adhering to the conventional development of the 'brotherhood' stories exemplified by the Titus–Gisippus story in Sir Thomas Elyot's *The Book of the Governor*. Thus Valentine hears Proteus's brief repentance and forgives him his transgressions. Furthermore, as a proof of his sincerity he offers him Silvia (V.4.77–83):

> *Then I am paid;*
> *And once again I do receive thee honest.*
> *Who by repentance is not satisfied*
> *Is nor of heaven nor earth, for these are pleased;*
> *By penitence th'Eternal's wrath's appeased.*
> *And, that my love may appear plain and free,*
> *All that was mine in Silvia I give thee.*

Whether these lines represent an abridgement of a much fuller 'repentance episode', as some scholars have argued, cannot be determined with any certainty. What is undeniable, however, is the authentic Shakespearian ring and sentiment of lines 79–80, and that, therefore, the speech, even if it is the result of cutting, must contain within it at least an indication of the direction which the action originally took.

What is important in the whole episode, however, is not the strange silence of Silvia while her fate is being decided, nor the rapidity of Proteus's repentance, nor the 'caddishness' of Valentine's action by twentieth-century standards, nor the unsatisfactory nature of some of the verse. Rather, it is that the playwright is expecting too great a shift of receptivity in his audience. As has been pointed out earlier, for brief moments during the play he has managed to lift some of his creations out of the original Romance framework he adopted; and at this point his success in having done so will not allow them to be fitted back again into the two-dimensional mould. The Proteus we have followed through a half-credible struggle with self and a deluded degeneration into lustfulness, and the Julia who has been for substantial stretches of the play's action a convincing figure both psychologically and symbolically, are simply out of place in what is little more than a Romance tableau.

More important still is that the serious issues raised by the play, such as the double definition of love or the dichotomy between half-realized ideals and a testing reality, find neither their dramatic nor their aesthetic climax in this recourse to an unqualified presentation of a rigid narrative convention. It is a case of Shakespeare's emerging skill as a dramatist causing him to fail in the management of this essentially undramatic convention, even as John Lyly's more limited dramatic gifts enabled him to succeed in approximately the same mode. It was only much later, after a great deal of experience and further experimentation, that the playwright was able to use the Romance and Pastoral conventions (in plays like *The Tempest* or *The Winter's Tale*) in such a way as both to make their theatrical acceptance possible and to widen their boundaries enough to embrace his very personal vision of life.

In *The Two Gentlemen of Verona*, then, Shakespeare was unable to reconcile successfully the many oppositions in his dramatic material – oppositions between his desire to use Romance conventions to enlarge his range of dramatic reference in a way neo-Classical comedy did not allow and the consequent need credibly to juxtapose impossible ideals and observed reality; between the world of Petrarchan love rituals and values and his instinctive perception of the dangers inherent in these for the natural man; between the great goods of mercy, forgiveness, and truth and the difficulty of making these things appear attainable in dramatic terms by none-too-perfect individuals; and between a knowledge of the importance of concepts like true identity, clear vision, constancy, and right relationships, and the necessity of a dramatic projection, in an arranged pattern of experience, of the transformation that such values can work in men. But, although in no general sense successful, Shakespeare came near to achieving his aims in certain details, which is perhaps what makes the play a fascination to anyone interested in his comic achievement as a whole.

In the terminology of the litigious Elizabethan age, 'an earnest' was a small sum of money paid as guarantee of a much larger payment in the same coin at some future date. In this sense of the word, *The Two Gentlemen of Verona* may be considered the young Shakespeare's poetic and dramatic earnest of future comic success – and it is so in a way that *The Comedy of Errors* and *The Taming of the Shrew*, for all their more immediately obvious accomplishment and greater theatrical effectiveness, can never hope to be.

FURTHER READING

(1) *Editions and Editorial Problems*

The most readily available photographic reproduction of the original text of the play is to be found in the not always reliable facsimile of the Folio edited by H. Kökeritz and C. T. Prouty (1954). Several modern editions have been produced, among which may be mentioned those by R. W. Bond for the (old) Arden Shakespeare (1906), the commentary of which is still the best and fullest; by A. Quiller-Couch and J. Dover Wilson for the New Cambridge Edition (1921); by K. Young for the Yale Shakespeare (1924); and by M. R. Ridley for the New Temple Shakespeare (1935).

All of these editions contain discussions of the textual difficulties of the Folio; the fullest and most influential of these is Wilson's presentation of the case for the play's being an adaptation. This may be supplemented by the detailed analyses in W. W. Greg's *The Shakespeare First Folio* (1955) and C. Hinman's *The Printing and Proofreading of the First Folio of Shakespeare* (1963), and by the discussions of the major cruces in the text in Volume I of C. J. Sisson's *New Readings in Shakespeare* (1956) and in S. A. Tannenbaum's 'The New Cambridge Shakespeare and *The Two Gentlemen of Verona*' (*Shakespeare Association Bulletin*, XIII, 1938). Apart from Wilson, some scholars have hazarded guesses concerning what the hypothetical 'unadapted version' of the play may have contained; they include T. M. Parrott in his *Shakespearean Comedy* (1949) and G. B. Parks in 'The Development of *The Two Gentlemen of Verona*' (*The Huntington Library Bulletin*, XI, 1937).

(2) *Sources and Analogues*

The best general review of the possible sources and analogues of the play is to be found in Volume I of G. Bullough's *Narrative and Dramatic Sources of Shakespeare* (1957), which also prints a selection of the texts discussed. The text of Montemayor's 'Story of Felix and Felismena' is printed in full in *Elizabethan Love Stories*, edited by T. J. B. Spencer (Penguin Books, 1968). Some studies consider the play's relationship to separate works. T. P. Harrison, in 'Concerning *The Two Gentlemen of Verona* and Montemayor's *Diana*' (*Modern Language Notes*, XLI, 1926) and 'Shakespeare and Montemayor's *Diana*' (*University of Texas Studies in English*, VI, 1926), provides a defence of Shakespeare's use of Montemayor's *La Diana* against the claims that he relied on the lost play *Felix and Philiomena*. M. S. Allen discusses 'Brooke's *Romeus and Juliet* as a Source for the Valentine–Sylvia Plot in *The Two Gentlemen of Verona*' (*University of Texas Studies in English*, XVIII, 1938). The relationship between the play and the Italian drama *Gl'Ingannati* is examined by P. Reyher in '*The Two Gentlemen of Verona* et *Twelfth Night*, leurs sources communes' (*Revue de l'enseignement des langues vivantes*, XLI, 1924) and by R. Pruvost in '*The Two Gentlemen of Verona, Twelfth Night* et *Gl'Ingannati*' (*Études anglaises*, XIII, 1960).

Certain of Shakespeare's famous English contemporaries are considered to have had an influence on the writing of the play. D. Atkinson assesses that of Henry Wotton in 'The Source of *The Two Gentlemen of Verona*' (*Studies in Philology*, XLI, 1944), a topic which is also the subject of J. C. Pogue's '*The Two Gentlemen of Verona* and Henry Wotton's *A Courtlie Controversie of Cupid's Cautels*' (*Emporia State Research Studies*, X, 1926). Robert Greene's connexion is considered by T. H. McNeal in 'Who is Silvia – and Other Problems in the Greene–Shakespeare Relationship' (*Shakespeare Association Bulletin*, XIII, 1938) and by J. L. Tynan in 'The Influence of Greene on Shakespeare's Early Romance' (*Publications of the Modern Language Association of America*, XXVII, 1912). Ralph Sargent links 'Sir Thomas Elyot and the Integrity of *The Two Gentlemen of Verona*' (*Publications of the Modern Language Association of America*, LXV, 1950). R. W. Bond details the pervasive influence of John Lyly in his edition mentioned above and in *The Complete Works of John Lyly* (1902), and G. K. Hunter (*John Lyly: The Humanist as Courtier*, 1962) also discusses Shakespeare's debt to Lyly and provides a subtle comparison and contrast between the play's themes and techniques and some of Lyly's plays. On a more limited topic, J. A. Guinn sees various influences at work in Shakespeare's handling of the letter device in the first act (*University of Texas Studies in English*, XX, 1940).

(3) *Criticism*

Some critics usefully place the play in a broad context by examining it in the light of the conventions it employs. For example, Italian dramatic influences are discussed by Kathleen Lea in her *Italian Popular Comedy* (1934), and by O. J. Campbell, who sees in the machinery of disguise and pursuit traces of the *Commedia dell'Arte* (*Michigan Studies in Shakespeare, Milton and Donne*, 1925). The whole subject of foreign influences is considered in J. Wales's 'Shakespeare's Use of English and Foreign Elements in the Setting of *The Two Gentlemen of Verona*' (*Transactions of the Wisconsin Academy*, XXVII, 1932). T. W. Baldwin comments at length on the play's use of common structural and dramatic formulae in *Shakespere's Five-Act Structure* (1947).

Most of the criticism of the play has been characterized by an almost eighteenth-century freedom of vituperation; for example, S. A. Tannenbaum calls the story preposterous and the technique puerile, E. K. Chambers notes the sentimental bankruptcy (*Shakespeare: A Survey*, 1925), M. C. Bradbrook considers the play a colourless study in manners (*Shakespeare and Elizabethan Poetry*, 1951), D. A. Traversi calls it the most tedious play in the canon (*Shakespeare: The Early Comedies*, 1960), and E. M. W. Tillyard rates it as the least loved of Shakespeare's plays (*Shakespeare's Early Comedies*, 1965). But while most critics lament all or some aspects of the play, and take pleasure in pointing these out, perhaps the most sober assessment of its weaknesses – particularly the exact nature of the limitations of its techniques – as well as of its good qualities, is to be found in Stanley Wells's 'The Failure of *The Two Gentlemen of Verona*' (*Shakespeare Jahrbuch*, XCIX, 1963).

Some excuses have been made on the grounds that the play employs beliefs and conventions which are now little understood, particularly on the subjects of love and friendship, and attempts have been made to see it in the light of medieval concepts or Romance conventions. E. C. Pettet considers in detail the Romance elements (*Shakespeare and the Romance Tradition*, 1949), H. B. Charlton stresses the romantic and dehumanized atmosphere (*Shakespearian Comedy*, 1938), while Hardin Craig contrasts Shakespeare's treatment of the love–friendship theme with previous Renaissance versions in 'Shakespeare's Development as a Dramatist' (*Studies in Philology*, XXXIX, 1942). W. W. Lawrence reads the play in the light of the ideals of friendship preached in analogous contemporary works (*Shakespeare's Problem Comedies*, 1931); K. M. Thompson links the same theme to the conflict of love and honour which typified literary treatments of the medieval Courtly Love ethic ('Shakespeare's Romantic Comedies', *Publications of the Modern Language Association of America*, LXVII, 1952); and E. W. Talbert sees the incorporation of the Elizabethan concept of disciplined gentility (*Elizabethan Drama and Shakespeare's Early Plays*, 1963).

Certain features of the play have earned almost universal praise – especially the character of Julia, some of the lyrical passages, and the comic imagination which went into the creation of Launce and his prose idiom. M. C. Bradbrook, H. B. Charlton, Stanley Wells, D. A. Traversi, E. M. W. Tillyard, Sen Gupta (*Shakespearian Comedy*, 1950), and P. G. Phialas (*Shakespeare's Romantic Comedies*, 1966) all have interesting observations on these aspects of the play, but the best analysis of the dramatic and thematic interdependence of the comic and serious scenes and characters is Harold Brooks's 'Two Clowns in a Comedy (to Say Nothing of the Dog): Speed, Launce (and Crab) in *The Two Gentlemen of Verona*' (*Essays and Studies*, XVI, 1963).

The play has had some defenders who have seen deeper

matters lying behind the comic and Romance surface. For example, Ralph Sargent argues that the piece constitutes an immature but intelligent application of the principles of Romance to serious ideas about human relationships; Max Lüthi notes a central theme of self-discovery (*Shakespeares Dramen*, 1957); B. Evans sees in the play the triumph of innocence (*Shakespeare's Comedies*, 1960); and E. T. Sehrt observes a serious depiction of men at the mercy of fortune (*Wandlungen der Shakespeareschen Komödie*, 1961). Other writers concentrate on the central love situation, stressing different aspects of it. P. G. Phialas argues that forgiveness is the inmost meaning of love in the play, whereas John Danby sees love as a discipline by means of which the lover is admitted to a realm of values embodied in the woman loved ('Shakespearian Criticism and *The Two Gentlemen of Verona*', *Critical Quarterly*, II, 1960). John Vyvyan (*Shakespeare and the Rose of Love*, 1960) goes further than Danby, claiming that the play makes sense only when read as an allegory using the terminology of the *Roman de la Rose*, so that Silvia becomes the symbol of Eternal Platonic Beauty, the forest a Penitential Hermitage, and the Outlaws the rebel powers of Valentine's own nature. The concept of 'inward beauty' and its necessary recognition by the lover through the deceptiveness of outward appearances is suggested by John Russell Brown (*Shakespeare and his Comedies*, 1957), a theme also emphasized by D. A. Traversi.

Two critics of the play take it to be primarily satirical in intent: H. T. Price in 'Shakespeare as a Critic' (*Philological Quarterly*, XX, 1941) insists that it is a parody of Romance, and Clifford Leech (*Twelfth Night and Shakespearian Comedy*, 1965) argues that it indirectly mocks the conventions of ideal friendship and romantic love, chiefly by the parallelism and interplay of characters and situations.

The language and style of the play are discussed by G. Wilson Knight (*The Shakespearian Tempest*, 1932), who tends to overemphasize the sadness implicit in the metaphors, and by M. Van Doren (*Shakespeare*, 1939). E. M. W. Tillyard also has some perceptive comments on the nature of the verse at certain points in the play and suggests that it is Shakespeare's interest in dramatic techniques that imposes a special kind of unity on the play.

Some special topics which have received attention include studies of the play's ending from S. A. Small (*Publications of the Modern Language Association of America*, XLVIII, 1933) and from Alwin Thaler in 'Shakespeare and the Unhappy Happy Ending' (*Publications of the Modern Language Association of America*, XLII, 1927). The character of Proteus is discussed by T. A. Perry who sees him transformed by travel into a decadent Italian courtier in 'Proteus, Wry-Transformed Traveller' (*Shakespeare Quarterly*, V, 1954), and also by W. O. Scott who argues that Shakespeare relies heavily on the myth of Proteus to embody the theme of identity with its contrast between the real and false selves (*Shakespeare Studies*, I, 1965). The emerging materials which were to be characteristic of Shakespeare's later comedies are isolated by J. Dover Wilson (*Shakespeare's Happy Comedies*, 1962).

The following studies contain incidental comments of interest on the play: G. Gordon, *Shakespearian Comedy* (1944); D. L. Stevenson, *The Love-Game Comedy* (1946); N. Frye, 'The Argument of Comedy' (*English Institute Studies*, 1948); D. Stauffer, *Shakespeare's World of Images* (1949); N. Coghill, 'The Basis of Shakespearian Comedy' (*Essays and Studies*, 1950); N. Frye, 'Characterization in Shakespearian Comedy' (*Shakespeare Quarterly*, IV, 1953); M. Doran, *Endeavors of Art* (1954); M. Praz, 'Shakespeare's Italy' (*Shakespeare Survey*, VII, 1954); M. C. Bradbrook, *The Growth and Structure of Elizabethan Comedy* (1955); G. Bush, *Shakespeare and the Natural Condition* (1956); H. Jenkins, 'Shakespeare's *Twelfth Night*' (*Rice Institute Pamphlet*, XLV, 1959); and A. Righter, *Shakespeare and the Idea of the Play* (1962).

THE TWO GENTLEMEN
OF VERONA

THE CHARACTERS IN THE PLAY

THE DUKE OF MILAN
SILVIA, his daughter and the beloved of Valentine
THURIO, a foolish suitor for Silvia's hand
EGLAMOUR, Silvia's accomplice in her flight from Milan
PROTEUS ⎫
VALENTINE ⎭ the two gentlemen of Verona
JULIA, the beloved of Proteus, later disguised as
   SEBASTIAN, a page
ANTONIO, father of Proteus
LUCETTA, waiting-woman of Julia
SPEED, servant of Valentine
LAUNCE, servant of Proteus
PANTHINO, servant of Antonio
Host of the Inn where Julia lodges in Milan
Outlaws, led by Valentine during his banishment
Servants
Musicians
Attendants

VALENTINE

  Cease to persuade, my loving Proteus;
  Home-keeping youth have ever homely wits.
  Were't not affection chains thy tender days
  To the sweet glances of thy honoured love,
  I rather would entreat thy company
  To see the wonders of the world abroad
  Than, living dully sluggardized at home,
  Wear out thy youth with shapeless idleness.
  But, since thou lovest, love still, and thrive therein,
  Even as I would when I to love begin.   10

PROTEUS

  Wilt thou be gone? Sweet Valentine, adieu.
  Think on thy Proteus, when thou haply seest
  Some rare noteworthy object in thy travel.
  Wish me partaker in thy happiness,
  When thou dost meet good hap; and in thy danger –
  If ever danger do environ thee –
  Commend thy grievance to my holy prayers,
  For I will be thy beadsman, Valentine.

VALENTINE

  And on a love-book pray for my success?

PROTEUS

  Upon some book I love I'll pray for thee.   20

VALENTINE

  That's on some shallow story of deep love,
  How young Leander crossed the Hellespont.

PROTEUS

That's a deep story of a deeper love,
For he was more than over-shoes in love.

VALENTINE

'Tis true; for you are over-boots in love,
And yet you never swam the Hellespont.

PROTEUS

Over the boots? Nay, give me not the boots.

VALENTINE

No, I will not; for it boots thee not.

PROTEUS   What?

VALENTINE

To be in love, where scorn is bought with groans;
30   Coy looks, with heart-sore sighs; one fading moment's
            mirth,
With twenty, watchful, weary, tedious nights;
If haply won, perhaps a hapless gain;
If lost, why then a grievous labour won;
However, but a folly bought with wit,
Or else a wit by folly vanquishèd.

PROTEUS

So, by your circumstance, you call me fool?

VALENTINE

So, by your circumstance, I fear you'll prove.

PROTEUS

'Tis Love you cavil at; I am not Love.

VALENTINE

Love is your master, for he masters you;
40   And he that is so yokèd by a fool,
Methinks should not be chronicled for wise.

PROTEUS

Yet writers say, as in the sweetest bud
The eating canker dwells, so eating love
Inhabits in the finest wits of all.

VALENTINE

    And writers say, as the most forward bud
    Is eaten by the canker ere it blow,
    Even so by love the young and tender wit
    Is turned to folly, blasting in the bud,
    Losing his verdure even in the prime,
    And all the fair effects of future hopes.   50
    But wherefore waste I time to counsel thee
    That art a votary to fond desire?
    Once more adieu. My father at the road
    Expects my coming, there to see me shipped.

PROTEUS

    And thither will I bring thee, Valentine.

VALENTINE

    Sweet Proteus, no; now let us take our leave.
    To Milan let me hear from thee by letters
    Of thy success in love, and what news else
    Betideth here in absence of thy friend;
    And I likewise will visit thee with mine.   60

PROTEUS

    All happiness bechance to thee in Milan.

VALENTINE

    As much to you at home. And so farewell.   *Exit*

PROTEUS

    He after honour hunts, I after love.
    He leaves his friends to dignify them more;
    I leave myself, my friends, and all for love.
    Thou, Julia, thou hast metamorphosed me,
    Made me neglect my studies, lose my time,
    War with good counsel, set the world at naught;
    Made wit with musing weak, heart sick with thought.
        Enter Speed

SPEED

    Sir Proteus, save you! Saw you my master?   70

PROTEUS

But now he parted hence to embark for Milan.

SPEED

Twenty to one then he is shipped already,
And I have played the sheep in losing him.

PROTEUS

Indeed, a sheep doth very often stray,
An if the shepherd be a while away.

SPEED You conclude that my master is a shepherd then,
and I a sheep?

PROTEUS I do.

SPEED Why then, my horns are his horns, whether I wake
80 or sleep.

PROTEUS A silly answer, and fitting well a sheep.

SPEED This proves me still a sheep.

PROTEUS True; and thy master a shepherd.

SPEED Nay, that I can deny by a circumstance.

PROTEUS It shall go hard but I'll prove it by another.

SPEED The shepherd seeks the sheep, and not the sheep
the shepherd; but I seek my master, and my master
seeks not me. Therefore I am no sheep.

PROTEUS The sheep for fodder follow the shepherd; the
90 shepherd for food follows not the sheep. Thou for
wages followest thy master, thy master for wages follows
not thee. Therefore thou art a sheep.

SPEED Such another proof will make me cry, 'baa'.

PROTEUS But dost thou hear? Gavest thou my letter to
Julia?

SPEED Ay, sir. I, a lost mutton, gave your letter to her,
a laced mutton; and she, a laced mutton, gave me, a lost
mutton, nothing for my labour.

PROTEUS Here's too small a pasture for such store of
100 muttons.

SPEED If the ground be overcharged, you were best stick
her.

PROTEUS Nay, in that you are astray; 'twere best pound
you.

SPEED Nay, sir, less than a pound shall serve me for
carrying your letter.

PROTEUS You mistake; I mean the pound – a pinfold.

SPEED

From a pound to a pin? Fold it over and over,
'Tis threefold too little for carrying a letter to your lover.

PROTEUS But what said she?   110

    Speed nods

A nod?

SPEED Ay.

PROTEUS Nod-ay? Why, that's noddy.

SPEED You mistook, sir. I say she did nod; and you ask
me if she did nod, and I say 'Ay'.

PROTEUS And that set together is 'noddy'.

SPEED Now you have taken the pains to set it together,
take it for your pains.

PROTEUS No, no; you shall have it for bearing the letter.

SPEED Well, I perceive I must be fain to bear with you. 120

PROTEUS Why, sir, how do you bear with me?

SPEED Marry, sir, the letter very orderly, having nothing
but the word 'noddy' for my pains.

PROTEUS Beshrew me, but you have a quick wit.

SPEED And yet it cannot overtake your slow purse.

PROTEUS Come, come, open the matter in brief; what
said she?

SPEED Open your purse, that the money and the matter
may be both at once delivered.

PROTEUS Well, sir, here is for your pains.   130

    He gives Speed money

What said she?

SPEED Truly, sir, I think you'll hardly win her.

PROTEUS Why? Couldst thou perceive so much from her?

SPEED Sir, I could perceive nothing at all from her; no, not so much as a ducat for delivering your letter; and being so hard to me that brought your mind, I fear she'll prove as hard to you in telling your mind. Give her no token but stones, for she's as hard as steel.

140 PROTEUS What said she? Nothing?

SPEED No, not so much as 'Take this for thy pains'. To testify your bounty, I thank you, you have testerned me; in requital whereof, henceforth carry your letters yourself. And so, sir, I'll commend you to my master.

Exit

PROTEUS

Go, go, be gone, to save your ship from wreck,
Which cannot perish, having thee aboard,
Being destined to a drier death on shore.
I must go send some better messenger.
I fear my Julia would not deign my lines,
150 Receiving them from such a worthless post.   *Exit*

I.2   *Enter Julia and Lucetta*

JULIA

But say, Lucetta, now we are alone,
Wouldst thou then counsel me to fall in love?

LUCETTA

Ay, madam, so you stumble not unheedfully.

JULIA

Of all the fair resort of gentlemen
That every day with parle encounter me,

In thy opinion which is worthiest love?

LUCETTA
Please you repeat their names, I'll show my mind
According to my shallow simple skill.

JULIA
What thinkest thou of the fair Sir Eglamour?

LUCETTA
As of a knight well-spoken, neat, and fine;
But, were I you, he never should be mine.

JULIA
What thinkest thou of the rich Mercatio?

LUCETTA
Well of his wealth; but of himself, so so.

JULIA
What thinkest thou of the gentle Proteus?

LUCETTA
Lord, lord, to see what folly reigns in us!

JULIA
How now, what means this passion at his name?

LUCETTA
Pardon, dear madam; 'tis a passing shame
That I, unworthy body as I am,
Should censure thus on lovely gentlemen.

JULIA
Why not on Proteus, as of all the rest?

LUCETTA
Then thus: of many good, I think him best.

JULIA
Your reason?

LUCETTA
I have no other but a woman's reason:
I think him so, because I think him so.

JULIA
And wouldst thou have me cast my love on him?

LUCETTA

Ay, if you thought your love not cast away.

JULIA

Why, he, of all the rest, hath never moved me.

LUCETTA

Yet he, of all the rest, I think best loves ye.

JULIA

His little speaking shows his love but small.

LUCETTA

30 Fire that's closest kept burns most of all.

JULIA

They do not love that do not show their love.

LUCETTA

O, they love least that let men know their love.

JULIA

I would I knew his mind.

LUCETTA

Peruse this paper, madam.

JULIA *(reads)*

To Julia. – Say, from whom?

LUCETTA

That the contents will show.

JULIA

Say, say, who gave it thee?

LUCETTA

Sir Valentine's page; and sent, I think, from Proteus.

He would have given it you; but I, being in the way,

40 Did in your name receive it; pardon the fault, I pray.

JULIA

Now, by my modesty, a goodly broker!

Dare you presume to harbour wanton lines?

To whisper and conspire against my youth?

Now, trust me, 'tis an office of great worth,

And you an officer fit for the place.

There take the paper. See it be returned,
Or else return no more into my sight.

LUCETTA

To plead for love deserves more fee than hate.

JULIA

Will ye be gone?

LUCETTA   That you may ruminate.   *Exit*

JULIA

And yet I would I had o'erlooked the letter.   50
It were a shame to call her back again,
And pray her to a fault for which I chid her.
What 'fool is she, that knows I am a maid,
And would not force the letter to my view,
Since maids, in modesty, say no to that
Which they would have the profferer construe ay.
Fie, fie! How wayward is this foolish love,
That, like a testy babe, will scratch the nurse,
And presently, all humbled, kiss the rod.
How churlishly I chid Lucetta hence,   60
When willingly I would have had her here.
How angerly I taught my brow to frown,
When inward joy enforced my heart to smile.
My penance is to call Lucetta back
And ask remission for my folly past.
What ho! Lucetta!

     Enter Lucetta

LUCETTA   What would your ladyship?

JULIA

Is't near dinner-time?

LUCETTA   I would it were,
That you might kill your stomach on your meat,
And not upon your maid.

     She drops and picks up the letter

59

JULIA

70 What is't that you took up so gingerly?

LUCETTA

Nothing.

JULIA

Why didst thou stoop then?

LUCETTA

To take a paper up that I let fall.

JULIA

And is that paper nothing?

LUCETTA

Nothing concerning me.

JULIA

Then let it lie for those that it concerns.

LUCETTA

Madam, it will not lie where it concerns,
Unless it have a false interpreter.

JULIA

Some love of yours hath writ to you in rhyme.

LUCETTA

80 That I might sing it, madam, to a tune.
Give me a note; your ladyship can set.

JULIA

As little by such toys as may be possible.
Best sing it to the tune of 'Light o'love'.

LUCETTA

It is too heavy for so light a tune.

JULIA

Heavy? Belike it hath some burden then?

LUCETTA

Ay, and melodious were it, would you sing it.

JULIA

And why not you?

LUCETTA   I cannot reach so high.

JULIA

Let's see your song. How now, minion!

Julia snatches at the letter which Lucetta retains

LUCETTA

Keep tune there still, so you will sing it out;

And yet methinks I do not like this tune.   90

Julia seizes the letter

JULIA

You do not?

LUCETTA   No, madam; it is too sharp.

JULIA

You, minion, are too saucy.

LUCETTA

Nay, now you are too flat;

And mar the concord with too harsh a descant.

There wanteth but a mean to fill your song.

JULIA

The mean is drowned with your unruly bass.

LUCETTA

Indeed, I bid the bass for Proteus.

JULIA

This babble shall not henceforth trouble me.

Here is a coil with protestation.

She tears the letter

Go, get you gone, and let the papers lie.   100

You would be fingering them, to anger me.

LUCETTA (*aside*)

She makes it strange, but she would be best pleased

To be so angered with another letter.   *Exit*

JULIA

Nay, would I were so angered with the same!

O, hateful hands, to tear such loving words.

Injurious wasps, to feed on such sweet honey,

And kill the bees that yield it with your stings.

I'll kiss each several paper for amends.
Look, here is writ, *kind Julia*. Unkind Julia,
110   As in revenge of thy ingratitude,
I throw thy name against the bruising stones,
Trampling contemptuously on thy disdain.
And here is writ, *love-wounded Proteus*.
Poor wounded name, my bosom, as a bed,
Shall lodge thee till thy wound be throughly healed;
And thus I search it with a sovereign kiss.
But twice or thrice was Proteus written down.
Be calm, good wind, blow not a word away
Till I have found each letter in the letter,
120   Except mine own name. That some whirlwind bear
Unto a ragged, fearful, hanging rock,
And throw it thence into the raging sea.
Lo, here in one line is his name twice writ:
Poor, forlorn Proteus, passionate Proteus,
To the sweet Julia. That I'll tear away;
And yet I will not, sith so prettily
He couples it to his complaining names.
Thus will I fold them one upon another.
Now kiss, embrace, contend, do what you will.
    Enter Lucetta

LUCETTA
130   Madam,
Dinner is ready, and your father stays.

JULIA
Well, let us go.

LUCETTA
What, shall these papers lie like tell-tales here?

JULIA
If you respect them, best to take them up.

LUCETTA
Nay, I was taken up for laying them down.

Yet here they shall not lie for catching cold.
  She picks up the pieces of the letter

JULIA
  I see you have a month's mind to them.

LUCETTA
  Ay, madam, you may say what sights you see;
  I see things too, although you judge I wink.

JULIA
  Come, come, will't please you go?   *Exeunt* 140

  Enter Antonio and Panthino   I.3

ANTONIO
  Tell me, Panthino, what sad talk was that
  Wherewith my brother held you in the cloister?

PANTHINO
  'Twas of his nephew Proteus, your son.

ANTONIO
  Why, what of him?

PANTHINO   He wondered that your lordship
  Would suffer him to spend his youth at home,
  While other men, of slender reputation,
  Put forth their sons to seek preferment out:
  Some to the wars to try their fortune there;
  Some to discover islands far away;
  Some to the studious universities.   10
  For any or for all these exercises
  He said that Proteus your son was meet,
  And did request me to importune you
  To let him spend his time no more at home,
  Which would be great impeachment to his age,
  In having known no travel in his youth.

ANTONIO
  Nor needest thou much importune me to that

Whereon this month I have been hammering.
I have considered well his loss of time,
20 And how he cannot be a perfect man,
Not being tried and tutored in the world.
Experience is by industry achieved,
And perfected by the swift course of time.
Then tell me, whither were I best to send him?

PANTHINO
I think your lordship is not ignorant
How his companion, youthful Valentine,
Attends the Emperor in his royal court.

ANTONIO
I know it well.

PANTHINO
'Twere good, I think, your lordship sent him thither.
30 There shall he practise tilts and tournaments,
Hear sweet discourse, converse with noblemen,
And be in eye of every exercise
Worthy his youth and nobleness of birth.

ANTONIO
I like thy counsel; well hast thou advised;
And that thou mayst perceive how well I like it,
The execution of it shall make known.
Even with the speediest expedition
I will dispatch him to the Emperor's court.

PANTHINO
Tomorrow, may it please you, Don Alphonso
40 With other gentlemen of good esteem
Are journeying to salute the Emperor,
And to commend their service to his will.

ANTONIO
Good company; with them shall Proteus go.
Enter Proteus, reading a letter
And in good time; now will we break with him.

64

PROTEUS (*aside*)
Sweet love, sweet lines, sweet life!
Here is her hand, the agent of her heart;
Here is her oath for love, her honour's pawn.
O, that our fathers would applaud our loves,
To seal our happiness with their consents!
O heavenly Julia!   50

ANTONIO
How now? What letter are you reading there?

PROTEUS
May't please your lordship, 'tis a word or two
Of commendations sent from Valentine,
Delivered by a friend that came from him.

ANTONIO
Lend me the letter. Let me see what news.

PROTEUS
There is no news, my lord, but that he writes
How happily he lives, how well beloved,
And daily gracèd by the Emperor;
Wishing me with him, partner of his fortune.

ANTONIO
And how stand you affected to his wish?   60

PROTEUS
As one relying on your lordship's will,
And not depending on his friendly wish.

ANTONIO
My will is something sorted with his wish.
Muse not that I thus suddenly proceed;
For what I will, I will, and there an end.
I am resolved that thou shalt spend some time
With Valentinus in the Emperor's court.
What maintenance he from his friends receives,
Like exhibition thou shalt have from me.
Tomorrow be in readiness to go.   70

65

Excuse it not, for I am peremptory.

PROTEUS

My lord, I cannot be so soon provided.
Please you deliberate a day or two.

ANTONIO

Look what thou wantest shall be sent after thee.
No more of stay; tomorrow thou must go.
Come on, Panthino; you shall be employed
To hasten on his expedition.

Exeunt Antonio and Panthino

PROTEUS

Thus have I shunned the fire for fear of burning,
And drenched me in the sea, where I am drowned.
80 I feared to show my father Julia's letter,
Lest he should take exceptions to my love,
And with the vantage of mine own excuse
Hath he excepted most against my love.
O, how this spring of love resembleth
    The uncertain glory of an April day,
Which now shows all the beauty of the sun,
    And by and by a cloud takes all away.
    Enter Panthino

PANTHINO

Sir Proteus, your father calls for you.
    He is in haste; therefore, I pray you go.

PROTEUS

90 Why, this it is; my heart accords thereto,
    And yet a thousand times it answers, 'No.' *Exeunt*

✳

SPEED

Sir, your glove.

VALENTINE   Not mine. My gloves are on.

SPEED

Why then, this may be yours, for this is but one.

VALENTINE

Ha! Let me see. Ay, give it me, it's mine.

Sweet ornament that decks a thing divine.

Ah, Silvia, Silvia!

SPEED Madam Silvia! Madam Silvia!

VALENTINE How now, sirrah?

SPEED She is not within hearing, sir.

VALENTINE Why, sir, who bade you call her?

SPEED Your worship, sir, or else I mistook.   10

VALENTINE Well, you'll still be too forward.

SPEED And yet I was last chidden for being too slow.

VALENTINE Go to, sir. Tell me, do you know Madam
   Silvia?

SPEED She that your worship loves?

VALENTINE Why, how know you that I am in love?

SPEED Marry, by these special marks: first, you have
   learned, like Sir Proteus, to wreathe your arms, like a
   malcontent; to relish a love-song, like a robin-redbreast;
   to walk alone, like one that had the pestilence; to sigh,   20
   like a schoolboy that had lost his A B C; to weep, like a
   young wench that had buried her grandam; to fast, like
   one that takes diet; to watch, like one that fears robbing;
   to speak puling, like a beggar at Hallowmas. You were
   wont, when you laughed, to crow like a cock; when you
   walked, to walk like one of the lions; when you fasted,
   it was presently after dinner; when you looked sadly, it
   was for want of money. And now you are metamor-

30 phosed with a mistress, that, when I look on you, I can
hardly think you my master.

VALENTINE Are all these things perceived in me?

SPEED They are all perceived without ye.

VALENTINE Without me? They cannot.

SPEED Without you? Nay, that's certain; for without you
were so simple, none else would. But you are so without
these follies, that these follies are within you, and shine
through you like the water in an urinal, that not an eye
that sees you but is a physician to comment on your
malady.

40 VALENTINE But tell me, dost thou know my lady Silvia?

SPEED She that you gaze on so, as she sits at supper?

VALENTINE Hast thou observed that? Even she I mean.

SPEED Why, sir, I know her not.

VALENTINE Dost thou know her by my gazing on her,
and yet knowest her not?

SPEED Is she not hard-favoured, sir?

VALENTINE Not so fair, boy, as well-favoured.

SPEED Sir, I know that well enough.

VALENTINE What dost thou know?

50 SPEED That she is not so fair as, of you, well favoured.

VALENTINE I mean that her beauty is exquisite, but her
favour infinite.

SPEED That's because the one is painted, and the other
out of all count.

VALENTINE How painted? And how out of count?

SPEED Marry, sir, so painted to make her fair, that no
man counts of her beauty.

VALENTINE How esteemest thou me? I account of her
beauty.

60 SPEED You never saw her since she was deformed.

VALENTINE How long hath she been deformed?

SPEED Ever since you loved her.

VALENTINE I have loved her ever since I saw her, and still I see her beautiful.

SPEED If you love her, you cannot see her.

VALENTINE Why?

SPEED Because Love is blind. O, that you had mine eyes, or your own eyes had the lights they were wont to have, when you chid at Sir Proteus for going ungartered!

VALENTINE What should I see then? 70

SPEED Your own present folly, and her passing deformity; for he, being in love, could not see to garter his hose; and you, being in love, cannot see to put on your hose.

VALENTINE Belike, boy, then you are in love; for last morning you could not see to wipe my shoes.

SPEED True, sir; I was in love with my bed. I thank you, you swinged me for my love, which makes me the bolder to chide you for yours.

VALENTINE In conclusion, I stand affected to her.

SPEED I would you were set, so your affection would 80 cease.

VALENTINE Last night she enjoined me to write some lines to one she loves.

SPEED And have you?

VALENTINE I have.

SPEED Are they not lamely writ?

VALENTINE No, boy, but as well as I can do them. Peace, here she comes.

Enter Silvia

SPEED (*aside*) O excellent motion! O exceeding puppet! Now will he interpret to her. 90

VALENTINE Madam and mistress, a thousand good morrows.

SPEED (*aside*) O, give ye good even! Here's a million of manners.

SILVIA Sir Valentine and servant, to you two thousand.

SPEED (*aside*) He should give her interest, and she gives it
 him.

VALENTINE

As you enjoined me, I have writ your letter
 Unto the secret nameless friend of yours;
100 Which I was much unwilling to proceed in,
 But for my duty to your ladyship.
 He gives her the letter

SILVIA I thank you, gentle servant, 'tis very clerkly done.

VALENTINE

Now trust me, madam, it came hardly off;
 For, being ignorant to whom it goes,
 I writ at random, very doubtfully.

SILVIA

Perchance you think too much of so much pains?

VALENTINE

No, madam; so it stead you, I will write,
 Please you command, a thousand times as much;
 And yet –

SILVIA

110 A pretty period! Well, I guess the sequel;
 And yet I will not name it; and yet I care not;
 And yet take this again;
 She offers him the letter
                              and yet I thank you,
 Meaning henceforth to trouble you no more.

SPEED (*aside*)

And yet you will; and yet, another 'yet'.

VALENTINE

What means your ladyship? Do you not like it?

SILVIA

Yes, yes; the lines are very quaintly writ;
 But, since unwillingly, take them again.

Nay, take them.
>   *She offers the letter again*

VALENTINE   Madam, they are for you.

SILVIA
Ay, ay; you writ them, sir, at my request,
But I will none of them; they are for you.   120
I would have had them writ more movingly.
>   *Valentine takes the letter*

VALENTINE
Please you, I'll write your ladyship another.

SILVIA
And when it's writ, for my sake read it over;
And if it please you, so; if not, why, so.

VALENTINE
If it please me, madam, what then?

SILVIA
Why, if it please you, take it for your labour.
And so, good morrow, servant.   *Exit*

SPEED (*aside*)
O jest unseen, inscrutable, invisible
As a nose on a man's face, or a weathercock on a steeple!
>   My master sues to her; and she hath taught her suitor, 130
>   He being her pupil, to become her tutor.
>   O excellent device! Was there ever heard a better,
>   That my master, being scribe, to himself should write
>   the letter?

VALENTINE How now, sir? What are you reasoning with
yourself?

SPEED Nay, I was rhyming; 'tis you that have the reason.

VALENTINE To do what?

SPEED To be a spokesman from Madam Silvia.

VALENTINE To whom?

SPEED To yourself. Why, she woos you by a figure.   140

VALENTINE What figure?

SPEED By a letter, I should say.

VALENTINE Why, she hath not writ to me.

SPEED What need she, when she hath made you write to yourself? Why, do you not perceive the jest?

VALENTINE No, believe me.

SPEED No believing you, indeed, sir. But did you perceive her earnest?

VALENTINE She gave me none, except an angry word.

150 SPEED Why, she hath given you a letter.

VALENTINE That's the letter I writ to her friend.

SPEED And that letter hath she delivered, and there an end.

VALENTINE I would it were no worse.

SPEED I'll warrant you, 'tis as well:

> For often have you writ to her; and she, in modesty,
> Or else for want of idle time, could not again reply;
> Or fearing else some messenger, that might her mind discover,
> Herself hath taught her love himself to write unto her lover.

160 All this I speak in print, for in print I found it. Why muse you, sir? 'Tis dinner-time.

VALENTINE I have dined.

SPEED Ay, but hearken, sir: though the chameleon Love can feed on the air, I am one that am nourished by my victuals, and would fain have meat. O, be not like your mistress; be moved, be moved.   *Exeunt*

II.2   *Enter Proteus and Julia*

PROTEUS

Have patience, gentle Julia.

JULIA

I must, where is no remedy.

PROTEUS

When possibly I can, I will return.

JULIA

If you turn not, you will return the sooner.
Keep this remembrance for thy Julia's sake.
She gives him a ring

PROTEUS

Why, then, we'll make exchange; here, take you this.
He gives her a ring

JULIA

And seal the bargain with a holy kiss.

PROTEUS

Here is my hand for my true constancy;
And when that hour o'erslips me in the day
Wherein I sigh not, Julia, for thy sake,   10
The next ensuing hour some foul mischance
Torment me for my love's forgetfulness!
My father stays my coming. Answer not.
The tide is now – nay, not thy tide of tears;
That tide will stay me longer than I should.
Julia, farewell. (*Exit Julia*) What, gone without a word?
Ay, so true love should do; it cannot speak,
For truth hath better deeds than words to grace it.
Enter Panthino

PANTHINO

Sir Proteus, you are stayed for.

PROTEUS   Go; I come.
(*Aside*) Alas, this parting strikes poor lovers dumb.   20
Exeunt

Enter Launce with his dog, Crab   II.3

LAUNCE Nay, 'twill be this hour ere I have done weeping;
all the kind of the Launces have this very fault. I have
received my proportion, like the prodigious son, and am

going with Sir Proteus to the Imperial's court. I think
Crab my dog be the sourest-natured dog that lives. My
mother weeping, my father wailing, my sister crying,
our maid howling, our cat wringing her hands, and all
our house in a great perplexity; yet did not this cruel-
hearted cur shed one tear. He is a stone, a very pebble-
stone, and has no more pity in him than a dog. A Jew
would have wept to have seen our parting. Why, my
grandam, having no eyes, look you, wept herself blind
at my parting. Nay, I'll show you the manner of it.
This shoe is my father. No, this left shoe is my father.
No, no, this left shoe is my mother. Nay, that cannot be
so neither. Yes, it is so, it is so; it hath the worser sole.
This shoe with the hole in it is my mother, and this my
father. A vengeance on't, there 'tis. Now, sir, this staff
is my sister; for, look you, she is as white as a lily, and
as small as a wand. This hat is Nan our maid. I am the
dog. No, the dog is himself, and I am the dog. O, the
dog is me, and I am myself. Ay, so, so. Now come I to
my father: 'Father, your blessing.' Now should not the
shoe speak a word for weeping. Now should I kiss my
father; well, he weeps on. Now come I to my mother.
O, that she could speak now like an old woman! Well,
I kiss her. Why, there 'tis; here's my mother's breath up
and down. Now come I to my sister. Mark the moan she
makes. Now the dog all this while sheds not a tear, nor
speaks a word; but see how I lay the dust with my tears.

Enter Panthino

PANTHINO Launce, away, away! Aboard! Thy master is
shipped, and thou art to post after with oars. What's the
matter? Why weepest thou, man? Away, ass, you'll lose
the tide, if you tarry any longer.

LAUNCE It is no matter if the tied were lost, for it is the
unkindest tied that ever any man tied.

PANTHINO What's the unkindest tide?

LAUNCE Why, he that's tied here, Crab, my dog.

PANTHINO Tut, man, I mean thou'lt lose the flood; and, in losing the flood, lose thy voyage; and, in losing thy voyage, lose thy master; and, in losing thy master, lose thy service; and, in losing thy service – Why dost thou stop my mouth? 40

LAUNCE For fear thou shouldst lose thy tongue.

PANTHINO Where should I lose my tongue?

LAUNCE In thy tale.

PANTHINO In my tail!

LAUNCE Lose the tide, and the voyage, and the master, and the service, and the tied. Why, man, if the river were dry, I am able to fill it with my tears. If the wind were down, I could drive the boat with my sighs. 50

PANTHINO Come, come away, man. I was sent to call thee.

LAUNCE Sir, call me what thou darest.

PANTHINO Wilt thou go?

LAUNCE Well, I will go.   *Exeunt*

Enter Silvia, Thurio, Valentine, and Speed   II.4

SILVIA Servant!

VALENTINE Mistress?

SPEED (*to Valentine*) Master, Sir Thurio frowns on you.

VALENTINE (*to Speed*) Ay, boy; it's for love.

SPEED (*to Valentine*) Not of you.

VALENTINE (*to Speed*) Of my mistress, then.

SPEED (*to Valentine*) 'Twere good you knocked him.

Exit

SILVIA Servant, you are sad.

VALENTINE Indeed, madam, I seem so.

THURIO Seem you that you are not?   10

VALENTINE Haply I do.

THURIO So do counterfeits.

VALENTINE So do you.

THURIO What seem I that I am not?

VALENTINE Wise.

THURIO What instance of the contrary?

VALENTINE Your folly.

THURIO And how quote you my folly?

VALENTINE I quote it in your jerkin.

20 THURIO My jerkin is a doublet.

VALENTINE Well, then, I'll double your folly.

THURIO How?

SILVIA What, angry, Sir Thurio? Do you change colour?

VALENTINE Give him leave, madam; he is a kind of chameleon.

THURIO That hath more mind to feed on your blood than live in your air.

VALENTINE You have said, sir.

THURIO Ay, sir, and done too, for this time.

30 VALENTINE I know it well, sir; you always end ere you begin.

SILVIA A fine volley of words, gentlemen, and quickly shot off.

VALENTINE 'Tis indeed, madam. We thank the giver.

SILVIA Who is that, servant?

VALENTINE Yourself, sweet lady; for you gave the fire. Sir Thurio borrows his wit from your ladyship's looks, and spends what he borrows kindly in your company.

THURIO Sir, if you spend word for word with me, I shall
40 make your wit bankrupt.

VALENTINE I know it well, sir; you have an exchequer of words, and, I think, no other treasure to give your followers; for it appears by their bare liveries that they live by your bare words.

Enter the Duke of Milan

SILVIA No more, gentlemen, no more! Here comes my
   father.

DUKE

   Now, daughter Silvia, you are hard beset.
   Sir Valentine, your father is in good health.
   What say you to a letter from your friends
   Of much good news?

VALENTINE   My lord, I will be thankful   50
   To any happy messenger from thence.

DUKE

   Know ye Don Antonio, your countryman?

VALENTINE

   Ay, my good lord, I know the gentleman
   To be of worth, and worthy estimation,
   And not without desert so well reputed.

DUKE

   Hath he not a son?

VALENTINE

   Ay, my good lord, a son that well deserves
   The honour and regard of such a father.

DUKE

   You know him well?

VALENTINE

   I know him as myself; for from our infancy   60
   We have conversed and spent our hours together;
   And though myself have been an idle truant,
   Omitting the sweet benefit of time
   To clothe mine age with angel-like perfection,
   Yet hath Sir Proteus – for that's his name –
   Made use and fair advantage of his days:
   His years but young, but his experience old;
   His head unmellowed, but his judgement ripe;
   And in a word, for far behind his worth

70 Comes all the praises that I now bestow,
    He is complete in feature and in mind,
    With all good grace to grace a gentleman.
DUKE
    Beshrew me, sir, but if he make this good,
    He is as worthy for an empress' love
    As meet to be an emperor's counsellor.
    Well, sir, this gentleman is come to me
    With commendation from great potentates,
    And here he means to spend his time awhile.
    I think 'tis no unwelcome news to you.
VALENTINE
80 Should I have wished a thing, it had been he.
DUKE
    Welcome him then according to his worth.
    Silvia, I speak to you, and you, Sir Thurio;
    For Valentine, I need not cite him to it.
    I will send him hither to you presently.   *Exit*
VALENTINE
    This is the gentleman I told your ladyship
    Had come along with me but that his mistress
    Did hold his eyes locked in her crystal looks.
SILVIA
    Belike that now she hath enfranchised them
    Upon some other pawn for fealty.
VALENTINE
90 Nay, sure, I think she holds them prisoners still.
SILVIA
    Nay, then, he should be blind; and, being blind,
    How could he see his way to seek out you?
VALENTINE
    Why, lady, Love hath twenty pair of eyes.
THURIO
    They say that Love hath not an eye at all.

VALENTINE

To see such lovers, Thurio, as yourself;
Upon a homely object Love can wink.

Enter Proteus

SILVIA

Have done, have done; here comes the gentleman.

VALENTINE

Welcome, dear Proteus! Mistress, I beseech you
Confirm his welcome with some special favour.

SILVIA

His worth is warrant for his welcome hither,   100
If this be he you oft have wished to hear from.

VALENTINE

Mistress, it is. Sweet lady, entertain him
To be my fellow-servant to your ladyship.

SILVIA

Too low a mistress for so high a servant.

PROTEUS

Not so, sweet lady; but too mean a servant
To have a look of such a worthy mistress.

VALENTINE

Leave off discourse of disability;
Sweet lady, entertain him for your servant.

PROTEUS

My duty will I boast of, nothing else.

SILVIA

And duty never yet did want his meed.   110
Servant, you are welcome to a worthless mistress.

PROTEUS

I'll die on him that says so but yourself.

SILVIA

That you are welcome?

PROTEUS   That you are worthless.

Enter a Servant

SERVANT

Madam, my lord your father would speak with you.

SILVIA

I wait upon his pleasure. (*Exit Servant*) Come, Sir
    Thurio,
Go with me. Once more, new servant, welcome.
I'll leave you to confer of home affairs;
When you have done, we look to hear from you.

PROTEUS

We'll both attend upon your ladyship.

Exeunt Silvia and Thurio

VALENTINE

120   Now, tell me, how do all from whence you came?

PROTEUS

Your friends are well, and have them much com-
    mended.

VALENTINE

And how do yours?

PROTEUS   I left them all in health.

VALENTINE

How does your lady, and how thrives your love?

PROTEUS

My tales of love were wont to weary you;
I know you joy not in a love-discourse.

VALENTINE

Ay, Proteus, but that life is altered now;
I have done penance for contemning Love,
Whose high imperious thoughts have punished me
With bitter fasts, with penitential groans,
130   With nightly tears, and daily heart-sore sighs;
For, in revenge of my contempt of love,
Love hath chased sleep from my enthrallèd eyes,
And made them watchers of mine own heart's sorrow.
O gentle Proteus, Love's a mighty lord,

And hath so humbled me as I confess
There is no woe to his correction,
Nor to his service no such joy on earth.
Now no discourse, except it be of love;
Now can I break my fast, dine, sup, and sleep,
Upon the very naked name of love.   140

PROTEUS
Enough; I read your fortune in your eye.
Was this the idol that you worship so?

VALENTINE
Even she; and is she not a heavenly saint?

PROTEUS
No; but she is an earthly paragon.

VALENTINE
Call her divine.

PROTEUS   I will not flatter her.

VALENTINE
O, flatter me; for love delights in praises.

PROTEUS
When I was sick, you gave me bitter pills,
And I must minister the like to you.

VALENTINE
Then speak the truth by her; if not divine,
Yet let her be a principality,   150
Sovereign to all the creatures on the earth.

PROTEUS
Except my mistress.

VALENTINE   Sweet, except not any;
Except thou wilt except against my love.

PROTEUS
Have I not reason to prefer mine own?

VALENTINE
And I will help thee to prefer her too:
She shall be dignified with this high honour –

To bear my lady's train, lest the base earth
Should from her vesture chance to steal a kiss,
And, of so great a favour growing proud,
160   Disdain to root the summer-swelling flower
And make rough winter everlastingly.

PROTEUS

Why, Valentine, what braggardism is this?

VALENTINE

Pardon me, Proteus, all I can is nothing
To her, whose worth makes other worthies nothing;
She is alone.

PROTEUS   Then let her alone.

VALENTINE

Not for the world! Why, man, she is mine own;
And I as rich in having such a jewel
As twenty seas, if all their sand were pearl,
The water nectar, and the rocks pure gold.
170   Forgive me, that I do not dream on thee,
Because thou seest me dote upon my love.
My foolish rival, that her father likes
Only for his possessions are so huge,
Is gone with her along; and I must after,
For love, thou knowest, is full of jealousy.

PROTEUS

But she loves you?

VALENTINE

Ay, and we are betrothed; nay more, our marriage-
    hour,
With all the cunning manner of our flight,
Determined of; how I must climb her window,
180   The ladder made of cords, and all the means
Plotted and 'greed on for my happiness.
Good Proteus, go with me to my chamber,
In these affairs to aid me with thy counsel.

PROTEUS

    Go on before; I shall inquire you forth.
    I must unto the road to disembark
    Some necessaries that I needs must use;
    And then I'll presently attend you.

VALENTINE

    Will you make haste?

PROTEUS

    I will.   *Exit Valentine*
    Even as one heat another heat expels,   190
    Or as one nail by strength drives out another,
    So the remembrance of my former love
    Is by a newer object quite forgotten.
    Is it mine eye, or Valentine's praise,
    Her true perfection, or my false transgression,
    That makes me reasonless to reason thus?
    She is fair; and so is Julia that I love –
    That I did love, for now my love is thawed;
    Which, like a waxen image 'gainst a fire,
    Bears no impression of the thing it was.   200
    Methinks my zeal to Valentine is cold,
    And that I love him not as I was wont.
    O, but I love his lady too too much!
    And that's the reason I love him so little.
    How shall I dote on her with more advice,
    That thus without advice begin to love her!
    'Tis but her picture I have yet beheld,
    And that hath dazzlèd my reason's light;
    But when I look on her perfections,
    There is no reason but I shall be blind.   210
    If I can check my erring love, I will;
    If not, to compass her I'll use my skill.   *Exit*

SPEED Launce! By mine honesty, welcome to Milan.

LAUNCE Forswear not thyself, sweet youth, for I am not welcome. I reckon this always, that a man is never undone till he be hanged, nor never welcome to a place till some certain shot be paid, and the hostess say, 'Welcome.'

SPEED Come on, you madcap; I'll to the alehouse with you presently; where, for one shot of five pence, thou shalt have five thousand welcomes. But, sirrah, how did thy master part with Madam Julia?

LAUNCE Marry, after they closed in earnest, they parted very fairly in jest.

SPEED But shall she marry him?

LAUNCE No.

SPEED How then? Shall he marry her?

LAUNCE No, neither.

SPEED What, are they broken?

LAUNCE No, they are both as whole as a fish.

SPEED Why then, how stands the matter with them?

LAUNCE Marry, thus: when it stands well with him, it stands well with her.

SPEED What an ass art thou! I understand thee not.

LAUNCE What a block art thou, that thou canst not! My staff understands me.

SPEED What thou sayest?

LAUNCE Ay, and what I do too; look there, I'll but lean, and my staff understands me.

SPEED It stands under thee, indeed.

LAUNCE Why, stand-under and under-stand is all one.

SPEED But tell me true, will't be a match?

LAUNCE Ask my dog. If he say ay, it will; if he say no, it will; if he shake his tail and say nothing, it will.

SPEED The conclusion is, then, that it will.

LAUNCE Thou shalt never get such a secret from me but by a parable.

SPEED 'Tis well that I get it so. But, Launce, how sayest thou that my master is become a notable lover?

LAUNCE I never knew him otherwise.

SPEED Than how?

LAUNCE A notable lubber, as thou reportest him to be. 40

SPEED Why, thou whoreson ass, thou mistakest me.

LAUNCE Why, fool, I meant not thee, I meant thy master.

SPEED I tell thee my master is become a hot lover.

LAUNCE Why, I tell thee, I care not though he burn himself in love. If thou wilt, go with me to the alehouse; if not, thou art an Hebrew, a Jew, and not worth the name of a Christian.

SPEED Why?

LAUNCE Because thou hast not so much charity in thee as 50
to go to the ale with a Christian. Wilt thou go?

SPEED At thy service.   *Exeunt*

Enter Proteus   II.6

PROTEUS

To leave my Julia, shall I be forsworn;
To love fair Silvia, shall I be forsworn;
To wrong my friend, I shall be much forsworn.
And e'en that power which gave me first my oath
Provokes me to this threefold perjury:
Love bade me swear, and Love bids me forswear.
O sweet-suggesting Love, if thou hast sinned,
Teach me, thy tempted subject, to excuse it!
At first I did adore a twinkling star,
But now I worship a celestial sun.   10
Unheedful vows may heedfully be broken;

85

And he wants wit that wants resolvèd will
To learn his wit t'exchange the bad for better.
Fie, fie, unreverend tongue, to call her bad
Whose sovereignty so oft thou hast preferred
With twenty thousand soul-confirming oaths!
I cannot leave to love, and yet I do;
But there I leave to love where I should love.
Julia I lose, and Valentine I lose;
20 If I keep them, I needs must lose myself;
If I lose them, thus find I by their loss:
For Valentine, myself; for Julia, Silvia.
I to myself am dearer than a friend,
For love is still most precious in itself;
And Silvia – witness heaven, that made her fair! –
Shows Julia but a swarthy Ethiope.
I will forget that Julia is alive,
Remembering that my love to her is dead;
And Valentine I'll hold an enemy,
30 Aiming at Silvia as a sweeter friend.
I cannot now prove constant to myself
Without some treachery used to Valentine.
This night he meaneth with a corded ladder
To climb celestial Silvia's chamber-window,
Myself in counsel, his competitor.
Now presently I'll give her father notice
Of their disguising and pretended flight,
Who, all enraged, will banish Valentine,
For Thurio he intends shall wed his daughter;
40 But Valentine being gone, I'll quickly cross
By some sly trick blunt Thurio's dull proceeding.
Love, lend me wings to make my purpose swift,
As thou hast lent me wit to plot this drift!   *Exit*

JULIA

    Counsel, Lucetta; gentle girl, assist me;
    And, e'en in kind love, I do conjure thee,
    Who art the table wherein all my thoughts
    Are visibly charactered and engraved,
    To lesson me and tell me some good mean
    How, with my honour, I may undertake
    A journey to my loving Proteus.

LUCETTA

    Alas, the way is wearisome and long!

JULIA

    A true-devoted pilgrim is not weary
    To measure kingdoms with his feeble steps;   10
    Much less shall she that hath Love's wings to fly,
    And when the flight is made to one so dear,
    Of such divine perfection as Sir Proteus.

LUCETTA

    Better forbear till Proteus make return.

JULIA

    O, knowest thou not his looks are my soul's food?
    Pity the dearth that I have pinèd in
    By longing for that food so long a time.
    Didst thou but know the inly touch of love,
    Thou wouldst as soon go kindle fire with snow
    As seek to quench the fire of love with words.   20

LUCETTA

    I do not seek to quench your love's hot fire,
    But qualify the fire's extreme rage,
    Lest it should burn above the bounds of reason.

JULIA

    The more thou dammest it up, the more it burns.
    The current that with gentle murmur glides,
    Thou knowest, being stopped, impatiently doth rage;

But when his fair course is not hinderèd,
He makes sweet music with th'enamelled stones,
Giving a gentle kiss to every sedge
30 He overtaketh in his pilgrimage;
And so by many winding nooks he strays,
With willing sport, to the wild ocean.
Then let me go, and hinder not my course.
I'll be as patient as a gentle stream,
And make a pastime of each weary step,
Till the last step have brought me to my love;
And there I'll rest as, after much turmoil,
A blessèd soul doth in Elysium.

LUCETTA
But in what habit will you go along?

JULIA
40 Not like a woman, for I would prevent
The loose encounters of lascivious men.
Gentle Lucetta, fit me with such weeds
As may beseem some well-reputed page.

LUCETTA
Why then, your ladyship must cut your hair.

JULIA
No, girl, I'll knit it up in silken strings
With twenty odd-conceited true-love knots –
To be fantastic may become a youth
Of greater time than I shall show to be.

LUCETTA
What fashion, madam, shall I make your breeches?

JULIA
50 That fits as well as, 'Tell me, good my lord,
What compass will you wear your farthingale?'
Why e'en what fashion thou best likes, Lucetta.

LUCETTA
You must needs have them with a codpiece, madam.

JULIA

    Out, out, Lucetta, that will be ill-favoured.

LUCETTA

    A round hose, madam, now's not worth a pin,
    Unless you have a codpiece to stick pins on.

JULIA

    Lucetta, as thou lovest me, let me have
    What thou thinkest meet, and is most mannerly.
    But tell me, wench, how will the world repute me
    For undertaking so unstaid a journey?   60
    I fear me it will make me scandalized.

LUCETTA

    If you think so, then stay at home and go not.

JULIA

    Nay, that I will not.

LUCETTA

    Then never dream on infamy, but go.
    If Proteus like your journey when you come,
    No matter who's displeased when you are gone.
    I fear me he will scarce be pleased withal.

JULIA

    That is the least, Lucetta, of my fear:
    A thousand oaths, an ocean of his tears,
    And instances of infinite of love,   70
    Warrant me welcome to my Proteus.

LUCETTA

    All these are servants to deceitful men.

JULIA

    Base men, that use them to so base effect!
    But truer stars did govern Proteus' birth;
    His words are bonds, his oaths are oracles,
    His love sincere, his thoughts immaculate,
    His tears pure messengers sent from his heart,
    His heart as far from fraud as heaven from earth.

LUCETTA

Pray heaven he prove so when you come to him!

JULIA

80 Now, as thou lovest me, do him not that wrong
To bear a hard opinion of his truth;
Only deserve my love by loving him;
And presently go with me to my chamber,
To take a note of what I stand in need of
To furnish me upon my longing journey.
All that is mine I leave at thy dispose,
My goods, my land, my reputation;
Only, in lieu thereof, dispatch me hence.
Come, answer not, but to it presently;
90 I am impatient of my tarriance. *Exeunt*

*

III.1 *Enter the Duke of Milan, Thurio, and Proteus*

DUKE

Sir Thurio, give us leave, I pray, awhile;
We have some secrets to confer about. *Exit Thurio*
Now, tell me, Proteus, what's your will with me?

PROTEUS

My gracious lord, that which I would discover
The law of friendship bids me to conceal,
But when I call to mind your gracious favours
Done to me, undeserving as I am,
My duty pricks me on to utter that
Which else no worldly good should draw from me.
10 Know, worthy prince, Sir Valentine, my friend,
This night intends to steal away your daughter;
Myself am one made privy to the plot.

I know you have determined to bestow her
On Thurio, whom your gentle daughter hates;
And should she thus be stolen away from you,
It would be much vexation to your age.
Thus, for my duty's sake, I rather chose
To cross my friend in his intended drift
Than, by concealing it, heap on your head
A pack of sorrows which would press you down,   20
Being unprevented, to your timeless grave.

DUKE

Proteus, I thank thee for thine honest care,
Which to requite, command me while I live.
This love of theirs myself have often seen,
Haply when they have judged me fast asleep,
And oftentimes have purposed to forbid
Sir Valentine her company and my court;
But, fearing lest my jealous aim might err,
And so, unworthily, disgrace the man –
A rashness that I ever yet have shunned –   30
I gave him gentle looks, thereby to find
That which thyself hast now disclosed to me.
And, that thou mayst perceive my fear of this,
Knowing that tender youth is soon suggested,
I nightly lodge her in an upper tower,
The key whereof myself have ever kept;
And thence she cannot be conveyed away.

PROTEUS

Know, noble lord, they have devised a mean
How he her chamber-window will ascend
And with a corded ladder fetch her down;   40
For which the youthful lover now is gone,
And this way comes he with it presently;
Where, if it please you, you may intercept him.
But, good my lord, do it so cunningly

That my discovery be not aimèd at;
For, love of you, not hate unto my friend,
Hath made me publisher of this pretence.

DUKE

Upon mine honour, he shall never know
That I had any light from thee of this.

PROTEUS

50 Adieu, my lord, Sir Valentine is coming. *Exit*
    Enter Valentine

DUKE

Sir Valentine, whither away so fast?

VALENTINE

Please it your grace, there is a messenger
That stays to bear my letters to my friends,
And I am going to deliver them.

DUKE

Be they of much import?

VALENTINE

The tenor of them doth but signify
My health and happy being at your court.

DUKE

Nay then, no matter; stay with me awhile;
I am to break with thee of some affairs
60 That touch me near, wherein thou must be secret.
'Tis not unknown to thee that I have sought
To match my friend Sir Thurio to my daughter.

VALENTINE

I know it well, my lord; and, sure, the match
Were rich and honourable; besides, the gentleman
Is full of virtue, bounty, worth, and qualities
Beseeming such a wife as your fair daughter.
Cannot your grace win her to fancy him?

DUKE

No, trust me; she is peevish, sullen, froward,

Proud, disobedient, stubborn, lacking duty;
Neither regarding that she is my child,   70
Nor fearing me as if I were her father;
And, may I say to thee, this pride of hers,
Upon advice, hath drawn my love from her;
And where I thought the remnant of mine age
Should have been cherished by her child-like duty,
I now am full resolved to take a wife
And turn her out to who will take her in.
Then let her beauty be her wedding-dower;
For me and my possessions she esteems not.

VALENTINE
What would your grace have me to do in this?   80

DUKE
There is a lady of Verona here
Whom I affect; but she is nice, and coy,
And naught esteems my agèd eloquence.
Now, therefore, would I have thee to my tutor –
For long agone I have forgot to court;
Besides, the fashion of the time is changed –
How and which way I may bestow myself
To be regarded in her sun-bright eye.

VALENTINE
Win her with gifts, if she respect not words;
Dumb jewels often in their silent kind   90
More than quick words do move a woman's mind.

DUKE
But she did scorn a present that I sent her.

VALENTINE
A woman sometime scorns what best contents her.
Send her another; never give her o'er;
For scorn at first makes after-love the more.
If she do frown, 'tis not in hate of you,
But rather to beget more love in you;

93

If she do chide, 'tis not to have you gone,
For why, the fools are mad if left alone.
100 Take no repulse, whatever she doth say;
For 'Get you gone', she doth not mean 'Away!'
Flatter and praise, commend, extol their graces;
Though ne'er so black, say they have angels' faces.
That man that hath a tongue, I say, is no man,
If with his tongue he cannot win a woman.

DUKE
But she I mean is promised by her friends
Unto a youthful gentleman of worth;
And kept severely from resort of men,
That no man hath access by day to her.

VALENTINE
110 Why then, I would resort to her by night.

DUKE
Ay, but the doors be locked, and keys kept safe,
That no man hath recourse to her by night.

VALENTINE
What lets but one may enter at her window?

DUKE
Her chamber is aloft, far from the ground,
And built so shelving that one cannot climb it
Without apparent hazard of his life.

VALENTINE
Why then, a ladder, quaintly made of cords,
To cast up with a pair of anchoring hooks,
Would serve to scale another Hero's tower,
120 So bold Leander would adventure it.

DUKE
Now, as thou art a gentleman of blood,
Advise me where I may have such a ladder.

VALENTINE
When would you use it? Pray, sir, tell me that.

DUKE

This very night; for Love is like a child,
That longs for every thing that he can come by.

VALENTINE

By seven o'clock I'll get you such a ladder.

DUKE

But, hark thee; I will go to her alone;
How shall I best convey the ladder thither?

VALENTINE

It will be light, my lord, that you may bear it
Under a cloak that is of any length.   130

DUKE

A cloak as long as thine will serve the turn?

VALENTINE

Ay, my good lord.

DUKE   Then let me see thy cloak;
I'll get me one of such another length.

VALENTINE

Why, any cloak will serve the turn, my lord.

DUKE

How shall I fashion me to wear a cloak?
I pray thee, let me feel thy cloak upon me.

> *He lifts Valentine's cloak and finds a letter and a
> rope-ladder*

What letter is this same? What's here? *To Silvia!*
And here an engine fit for my proceeding.
I'll be so bold to break the seal for once.

> *(He opens the letter and reads)*

My thoughts do harbour with my Silvia nightly,   140
* And slaves they are to me, that send them flying.*
O, could their master come and go as lightly,
* Himself would lodge where, senseless, they are lying!*
My herald thoughts in thy pure bosom rest them,
* While I, their king, that thither them importune,*

Do curse the grace that with such grace hath blessed them,
    Because myself do want my servants' fortune.
I curse myself, for they are sent by me,
That they should harbour where their lord should be.
150 What's here?
Silvia, this night I will enfranchise thee.
'Tis so; and here's the ladder for the purpose.
Why, Phaethon – for thou art Merops' son –
Wilt thou aspire to guide the heavenly car,
And with thy daring folly burn the world?
Wilt thou reach stars, because they shine on thee?
Go, base intruder, overweening slave,
Bestow thy fawning smiles on equal mates;
And think my patience, more than thy desert,
160 Is privilege for thy departure hence.
Thank me for this more than for all the favours
Which, all too much, I have bestowed on thee.
But if thou linger in my territories
Longer than swiftest expedition
Will give thee time to leave our royal court,
By heaven, my wrath shall far exceed the love
I ever bore my daughter or thyself.
Be gone; I will not hear thy vain excuse,
But, as thou lovest thy life, make speed from hence.

                             Exit

VALENTINE
170 And why not death, rather than living torment?
To die is to be banished from myself,
And Silvia is myself; banished from her
Is self from self – a deadly banishment.
What light is light, if Silvia be not seen?
What joy is joy, if Silvia be not by?
Unless it be to think that she is by,
And feed upon the shadow of perfection.

Except I be by Silvia in the night,
There is no music in the nightingale;
Unless I look on Silvia in the day,　　　　　　　180
There is no day for me to look upon.
She is my essence, and I leave to be,
If I be not by her fair influence
Fostered, illumined, cherished, kept alive.
I fly not death, to fly his deadly doom:
Tarry I here, I but attend on death;
But fly I hence, I fly away from life.

  Enter Proteus and Launce

PROTEUS Run, boy, run, run, and seek him out.
LAUNCE So-ho, so-ho!
PROTEUS What seest thou?　　　　　　　190
LAUNCE Him we go to find: there's not a hair on's head
 but 'tis a Valentine.
PROTEUS Valentine?
VALENTINE No.
PROTEUS Who then? His spirit?
VALENTINE Neither.
PROTEUS What then?
VALENTINE Nothing.
LAUNCE Can nothing speak? Master, shall I strike?
PROTEUS Who wouldst thou strike?　　　　　　　200
LAUNCE Nothing.
PROTEUS Villain, forbear.
LAUNCE Why, sir, I'll strike nothing. I pray you –
PROTEUS
 Sirrah, I say forbear. Friend Valentine, a word.
VALENTINE
 My ears are stopped and cannot hear good news,
 So much of bad already hath possessed them.
PROTEUS
 Then in dumb silence will I bury mine,

For they are harsh, untuneable, and bad.

VALENTINE

Is Silvia dead?

PROTEUS

210 No, Valentine.

VALENTINE

No Valentine, indeed, for sacred Silvia.
Hath she forsworn me?

PROTEUS

No, Valentine.

VALENTINE

No Valentine, if Silvia have forsworn me.
What is your news?

LAUNCE Sir, there is a proclamation that you are vanished.

PROTEUS

That thou art banishèd – O, that's the news! –
From hence, from Silvia, and from me thy friend.

VALENTINE

O, I have fed upon this woe already,
220 And now excess of it will make me surfeit.
Doth Silvia know that I am banishèd?

PROTEUS

Ay, ay; and she hath offered to the doom –
Which, unreversed, stands in effectual force –
A sea of melting pearl, which some call tears;
Those at her father's churlish feet she tendered;
With them, upon her knees, her humble self,
Wringing her hands, whose whiteness so became them
As if but now they waxèd pale for woe.
But neither bended knees, pure hands held up,
230 Sad sighs, deep groans, nor silver-shedding tears,
Could penetrate her uncompassionate sire –
But Valentine, if he be ta'en, must die.

Besides, her intercession chafed him so,
When she for thy repeal was suppliant,
That to close prison he commanded her,
With many bitter threats of biding there.

VALENTINE

No more; unless the next word that thou speakest
Have some malignant power upon my life;
If so, I pray thee breathe it in mine ear,
As ending anthem of my endless dolour.   240

PROTEUS

Cease to lament for that thou canst not help,
And study help for that which thou lamentest.
Time is the nurse and breeder of all good;
Here, if thou stay, thou canst not see thy love;
Besides, thy staying will abridge thy life.
Hope is a lover's staff; walk hence with that,
And manage it against despairing thoughts.
Thy letters may be here, though thou art hence,
Which, being writ to me, shall be delivered
Even in the milk-white bosom of thy love.   250
The time now serves not to expostulate.
Come I'll convey thee through the city gate;
And, ere I part with thee, confer at large
Of all that may concern thy love affairs.
As thou lovest Silvia, though not for thyself,
Regard thy danger, and along with me.

VALENTINE

I pray thee, Launce, an if thou seest my boy,
Bid him make haste and meet me at the Northgate.

PROTEUS

Go, sirrah, find him out. Come, Valentine.

VALENTINE

O my dear Silvia! Hapless Valentine!   260

Exeunt Valentine and Proteus

99

LAUNCE I am but a fool, look you, and yet I have the wit to think my master is a kind of a knave; but that's all one if he be but one knave. He lives not now that knows me to be in love; yet I am in love; but a team of horse shall not pluck that from me; nor who 'tis I love; and yet 'tis a woman; but what woman I will not tell myself; and yet 'tis a milkmaid; yet 'tis not a maid, for she hath had gossips; yet 'tis a maid, for she is her master's maid and serves for wages. She hath more qualities than a water-spaniel – which is much in a bare Christian.

He produces a paper

Here is the cate-log of her condition. *Imprimis: She can fetch and carry.* Why, a horse can do no more; nay, a horse cannot fetch, but only carry; therefore is she better than a jade. *Item: She can milk.* Look you, a sweet virtue in a maid with clean hands.

Enter Speed

SPEED How now, Signior Launce? What news with your mastership?

LAUNCE With my master's ship? Why, it is at sea.

SPEED Well, your old vice still: mistake the word. What news, then, in your paper?

LAUNCE The blackest news that ever thou heardest.

SPEED Why, man? How black?

LAUNCE Why, as black as ink.

SPEED Let me read them.

LAUNCE Fie on thee, jolt-head; thou canst not read.

SPEED Thou liest; I can.

LAUNCE I will try thee. Tell me this: who begot thee?

SPEED Marry, the son of my grandfather.

LAUNCE O illiterate loiterer! It was the son of thy grandmother. This proves that thou canst not read.

SPEED Come, fool, come; try me in thy paper.

LAUNCE There; and Saint Nicholas be thy speed!

He hands over the paper from which Speed reads

SPEED *Imprimis: She can milk.*

LAUNCE Ay, that she can.

SPEED *Item: She brews good ale.*

LAUNCE And thereof comes the proverb: 'Blessing of your heart, you brew good ale.'

SPEED *Item: She can sew.*

LAUNCE That's as much as to say, 'Can she so?'

SPEED *Item: She can knit.* 300

LAUNCE What need a man care for a stock with a wench, when she can knit him a stock?

SPEED *Item: She can wash and scour.*

LAUNCE A special virtue; for then she need not be washed and scoured.

SPEED *Item: She can spin.*

LAUNCE Then may I set the world on wheels, when she can spin for her living.

SPEED *Item: She hath many nameless virtues.*

LAUNCE That's as much as to say, bastard virtues; that 310 indeed know not their fathers, and therefore have no names.

SPEED Here follow her vices.

LAUNCE Close at the heels of her virtues.

SPEED *Item: She is not to be kissed fasting, in respect of her breath.*

LAUNCE Well, that fault may be mended with a breakfast. Read on.

SPEED *Item: She hath a sweet mouth.*

LAUNCE That makes amends for her sour breath. 320

SPEED *Item: She doth talk in her sleep.*

LAUNCE It's no matter for that; so she sleep not in her talk.

SPEED *Item: She is slow in words.*

LAUNCE O villain, that set this down among her vices!

To be slow in words is a woman's only virtue. I pray thee, out with't, and place it for her chief virtue.

SPEED *Item: She is proud.*

LAUNCE Out with that too; it was Eve's legacy, and cannot be ta'en from her.

SPEED *Item: She hath no teeth.*

LAUNCE I care not for that neither, because I love crusts.

SPEED *Item: She is curst.*

LAUNCE Well, the best is, she hath no teeth to bite.

SPEED *Item: She will often praise her liquor.*

LAUNCE If her liquor be good, she shall; if she will not, I will; for good things should be praised.

SPEED *Item: She is too liberal.*

LAUNCE Of her tongue she cannot, for that's writ down she is slow of; of her purse, she shall not, for that I'll keep shut. Now, of another thing she may, and that cannot I help. Well, proceed.

SPEED *Item: She hath more hair than wit, and more faults than hairs, and more wealth than faults.*

LAUNCE Stop there; I'll have her; she was mine and not mine twice or thrice in that last article. Rehearse that once more.

SPEED *Item: She hath more hair than wit –*

LAUNCE More hair than wit? It may be I'll prove it: the cover of the salt hides the salt, and therefore it is more than the salt; the hair that covers the wit is more than the wit, for the greater hides the less. What's next?

SPEED *And more faults than hairs –*

LAUNCE That's monstrous. O, that that were out!

SPEED *And more wealth than faults.*

LAUNCE Why, that word makes the faults gracious. Well, I'll have her; an if it be a match, as nothing is impossible –

SPEED What then?

LAUNCE Why, then will I tell thee – that thy master stays 360
for thee at the Northgate.

SPEED For me?

LAUNCE For thee! Ay, who art thou? He hath stayed for
a better man than thee.

SPEED And must I go to him?

LAUNCE Thou must run to him, for thou hast stayed so
long that going will scarce serve the turn.

SPEED Why didst not tell me sooner? Pox of your love
letters!   *He returns the paper to Launce. Exit*

LAUNCE Now will he be swinged for reading my letter. 370
An unmannerly slave, that will thrust himself into
secrets! I'll after, to rejoice in the boy's correction.

Exit

Enter the Duke of Milan and Thurio   III.2

DUKE
Sir Thurio, fear not but that she will love you
Now Valentine is banished from her sight.

THURIO
Since his exile she hath despised me most,
Forsworn my company, and railed at me,
That I am desperate of obtaining her.

DUKE
This weak impress of love is as a figure
Trenchèd in ice, which with an hour's heat
Dissolves to water, and doth lose his form.
A little time will melt her frozen thoughts,
And worthless Valentine shall be forgot.   10
    Enter Proteus
How now, Sir Proteus? Is your countryman,
According to our proclamation, gone?

PROTEUS
Gone, my good lord.

103

III.2

DUKE

My daughter takes his going grievously.

PROTEUS

A little time, my lord, will kill that grief.

DUKE

So I believe; but Thurio thinks not so.
Proteus, the good conceit I hold of thee –
For thou hast shown some sign of good desert –
Makes me the better to confer with thee.

PROTEUS

20 Longer than I prove loyal to your grace
Let me not live to look upon your grace.

DUKE

Thou knowest how willingly I would effect
The match between Sir Thurio and my daughter?

PROTEUS

I do, my lord.

DUKE

And also, I think, thou art not ignorant
How she opposes her against my will?

PROTEUS

She did, my lord, when Valentine was here.

DUKE

Ay, and perversely she persevers so.
What might we do to make the girl forget
30 The love of Valentine, and love Sir Thurio?

PROTEUS

The best way is to slander Valentine,
With falsehood, cowardice, and poor descent –
Three things that women highly hold in hate.

DUKE

Ay, but she'll think that it is spoke in hate.

PROTEUS

Ay, if his enemy deliver it;

Therefore it must with circumstance be spoken
By one whom she esteemeth as his friend.

DUKE
Then you must undertake to slander him.

PROTEUS
And that, my lord, I shall be loath to do:
'Tis an ill office for a gentleman,   40
Especially against his very friend.

DUKE
Where your good word cannot advantage him,
Your slander never can endamage him;
Therefore the office is indifferent,
Being entreated to it by your friend.

PROTEUS
You have prevailed, my lord; if I can do it
By aught that I can speak in his dispraise,
She shall not long continue love to him.
But say this weed her love from Valentine,
It follows not that she will love Sir Thurio.   50

THURIO
Therefore, as you unwind her love from him,
Lest it should ravel, and be good to none,
You must provide to bottom it on me;
Which must be done by praising me as much
As you in worth dispraise Sir Valentine.

DUKE
And, Proteus, we dare trust you in this kind,
Because we know, on Valentine's report,
You are already Love's firm votary,
And cannot soon revolt and change your mind.
Upon this warrant shall you have access   60
Where you with Silvia may confer at large –
For she is lumpish, heavy, melancholy,
And, for your friend's sake, will be glad of you –

    Where you may temper her, by your persuasion,
    To hate young Valentine and love my friend.

PROTEUS

    As much as I can do I will effect.
    But you, Sir Thurio, are not sharp enough;
    You must lay lime to tangle her desires
    By wailful sonnets, whose composèd rhymes
70   Should be full-fraught with serviceable vows.

DUKE

    Ay,
    Much is the force of heaven-bred poesy.

PROTEUS

    Say that upon the altar of her beauty
    You sacrifice your tears, your sighs, your heart;
    Write till your ink be dry, and with your tears
    Moist it again, and frame some feeling line
    That may discover such integrity;
    For Orpheus' lute was strung with poets' sinews,
    Whose golden touch could soften steel and stones,
80   Make tigers tame, and huge leviathans
    Forsake unsounded deeps to dance on sands.
    After your dire-lamenting elegies,
    Visit by night your lady's chamber-window
    With some sweet consort; to their instruments
    Tune a deploring dump – the night's dead silence
    Will well become such sweet complaining grievance.
    This, or else nothing, will inherit her.

DUKE

    This discipline shows thou hast been in love.

THURIO

    And thy advice this night I'll put in practice;
90   Therefore, sweet Proteus, my direction-giver,
    Let us into the city presently
    To sort some gentlemen well skilled in music.

I have a sonnet that will serve the turn
To give the onset to thy good advice.

DUKE

About it, gentlemen!

PROTEUS

We'll wait upon your grace till after supper,
And afterward determine our proceedings.

DUKE

Even now about it! I will pardon you.   *Exeunt*

*

Enter certain Outlaws   IV.1

FIRST OUTLAW

Fellows, stand fast; I see a passenger.

SECOND OUTLAW

If there be ten, shrink not, but down with 'em.
Enter Valentine and Speed

THIRD OUTLAW

Stand, sir, and throw us that you have about ye;
If not, we'll make you sit, and rifle you.

SPEED

Sir, we are undone; these are the villains
That all the travellers do fear so much.

VALENTINE

My friends –

FIRST OUTLAW

That's not so, sir; we are your enemies.

SECOND OUTLAW

Peace! We'll hear him.

THIRD OUTLAW

Ay, by my beard, will we; for he's a proper man.   10

VALENTINE

Then know that I have little wealth to lose;

IV.1

A man I am crossed with adversity;
My riches are these poor habiliments,
Of which, if you should here disfurnish me,
You take the sum and substance that I have.

SECOND OUTLAW
Whither travel you?

VALENTINE
To Verona.

FIRST OUTLAW
Whence came you?

VALENTINE
From Milan.

THIRD OUTLAW Have you long sojourned there?

VALENTINE
20 Some sixteen months, and longer might have stayed,
If crooked fortune had not thwarted me.

FIRST OUTLAW
What, were you banished thence?

VALENTINE
I was.

SECOND OUTLAW
For what offence?

VALENTINE
For that which now torments me to rehearse:
I killed a man, whose death I much repent;
But yet I slew him manfully in fight,
Without false vantage or base treachery.

FIRST OUTLAW
Why, ne'er repent it, if it were done so.
30 But were you banished for so small a fault?

VALENTINE
I was, and held me glad of such a doom.

SECOND OUTLAW
Have you the tongues?

VALENTINE

My youthful travel therein made me happy,
Or else I often had been miserable.

THIRD OUTLAW

By the bare scalp of Robin Hood's fat friar,
This fellow were a king for our wild faction!

FIRST OUTLAW

We'll have him. Sirs, a word.

The Outlaws draw aside to talk

SPEED Master, be one of them; it's an honourable kind of
thievery.

VALENTINE

Peace, villain!   40

SECOND OUTLAW Tell us this: have you anything to take
to?

VALENTINE

Nothing but my fortune.

THIRD OUTLAW

Know then that some of us are gentlemen,
Such as the fury of ungoverned youth
Thrust from the company of awful men;
Myself was from Verona banishèd
For practising to steal away a lady,
An heir, and near allied unto the Duke.

SECOND OUTLAW

And I from Mantua, for a gentleman   50
Who, in my mood, I stabbed unto the heart.

FIRST OUTLAW

And I for such like petty crimes as these.
But to the purpose – for we cite our faults
That they may hold excused our lawless lives;
And partly, seeing you are beautified
With goodly shape, and by your own report
A linguist, and a man of such perfection

As we do in our quality much want –

SECOND OUTLAW
Indeed, because you are a banished man,
60 Therefore, above the rest, we parley to you.
Are you content to be our general –
To make a virtue of necessity,
And live as we do in this wilderness?

THIRD OUTLAW
What sayst thou? Wilt thou be of our consort?
Say 'ay', and be the captain of us all.
We'll do thee homage, and be ruled by thee,
Love thee as our commander and our king.

FIRST OUTLAW
But if thou scorn our courtesy, thou diest.

SECOND OUTLAW
Thou shalt not live to brag what we have offered.

VALENTINE
70 I take your offer, and will live with you,
Provided that you do no outrages
On silly women or poor passengers.

THIRD OUTLAW
No, we detest such vile base practices.
Come, go with us; we'll bring thee to our crews,
And show thee all the treasure we have got;
Which, with ourselves, all rest at thy dispose. *Exeunt*

IV.2   *Enter Proteus*

PROTEUS
Already have I been false to Valentine,
And now I must be as unjust to Thurio;
Under the colour of commending him,
I have access my own love to prefer;
But Silvia is too fair, too true, too holy,

To be corrupted with my worthless gifts.
When I protest true loyalty to her,
She twits me with my falsehood to my friend;
When to her beauty I commend my vows,
She bids me think how I have been forsworn   10
In breaking faith with Julia, whom I loved;
And notwithstanding all her sudden quips,
The least whereof would quell a lover's hope,
Yet, spaniel-like, the more she spurns my love
The more it grows and fawneth on her still.

Enter Thurio and Musicians

But here comes Thurio. Now must we to her window,
And give some evening music to her ear.

THURIO
How now, Sir Proteus, are you crept before us?

PROTEUS
Ay, gentle Thurio; for you know that love
Will creep in service where it cannot go.   20

THURIO
Ay, but I hope, sir, that you love not here.

PROTEUS
Sir, but I do; or else I would be hence.

THURIO
Who? Silvia?

PROTEUS   Ay, Silvia – for your sake.

THURIO
I thank you for your own. Now, gentlemen,
Let's tune, and to it lustily awhile.

*Enter, some way off, the Host of the Inn, and Julia in
a page's costume*

HOST Now, my young guest, methinks you're allycholly;
I pray you, why is it?

JULIA Marry, mine host, because I cannot be merry.

HOST Come, we'll have you merry; I'll bring you where

30   you shall hear music, and see the gentleman that you
asked for.

JULIA But shall I hear him speak?

HOST Ay, that you shall.

JULIA That will be music.

The Musicians play

HOST Hark, hark!

JULIA Is he among these?

HOST Ay; but, peace! Let's hear 'em.

Song

Who is Silvia? What is she,
   That all our swains commend her?
40 Holy, fair, and wise is she;
   The heaven such grace did lend her,
That she might admirèd be.

Is she kind as she is fair?
   For beauty lives with kindness.
Love doth to her eyes repair,
   To help him of his blindness;
And, being helped, inhabits there.

Then to Silvia let us sing
   That Silvia is excelling;
50 She excels each mortal thing
   Upon the dull earth dwelling.
To her let us garlands bring.

HOST How now? Are you sadder than you were before?
How do you, man? The music likes you not.

JULIA You mistake; the musician likes me not.

HOST Why, my pretty youth?

JULIA He plays false, father.

HOST How? Out of tune on the strings?

JULIA Not so; but yet so false that he grieves my very
heart-strings.   60

HOST You have a quick ear.

JULIA Ay, I would I were deaf; it makes me have a slow
heart.

HOST I perceive you delight not in music.

JULIA Not a whit, when it jars so.

HOST Hark, what fine change is in the music!

JULIA Ay; that change is the spite.

HOST You would have them always play but one thing?

JULIA
I would always have one play but one thing.
But, host, doth this Sir Proteus, that we talk on,   70
Often resort unto this gentlewoman?

HOST I tell you what Launce, his man, told me: he loved
her out of all nick.

JULIA Where is Launce?

HOST Gone to seek his dog, which tomorrow, by his
master's command, he must carry for a present to his
lady.

JULIA
Peace! Stand aside; the company parts.

PROTEUS
Sir Thurio, fear not you; I will so plead
That you shall say my cunning drift excels.   80

THURIO
Where meet we?

PROTEUS   At Saint Gregory's Well.

THURIO   Farewell.
                                    Exeunt Thurio and Musicians
            Enter Silvia at an upstairs window

PROTEUS
Madam, good even to your ladyship.

SILVIA

I thank you for your music, gentlemen.
Who is that that spake?

PROTEUS

One, lady, if you knew his pure heart's truth,
You would quickly learn to know him by his voice.

SILVIA

Sir Proteus, as I take it.

PROTEUS

Sir Proteus, gentle lady, and your servant.

SILVIA

What's your will?

PROTEUS   That I may compass yours.

SILVIA

90   You have your wish; my will is even this,
That presently you hie you home to bed.
Thou subtle, perjured, false, disloyal man,
Thinkest thou I am so shallow, so conceitless,
To be seducèd by thy flattery
That hast deceived so many with thy vows?
Return, return, and make thy love amends.
For me – by this pale queen of night I swear –
I am so far from granting thy request
That I despise thee for thy wrongful suit;
100   And by and by intend to chide myself
Even for this time I spend in talking to thee.

PROTEUS

I grant, sweet love, that I did love a lady,
But she is dead.

JULIA (aside)   'Twere false, if I should speak it;
For I am sure she is not burièd.

SILVIA

Say that she be; yet Valentine thy friend
Survives, to whom, thyself art witness,

I am betrothed; and art thou not ashamed
To wrong him with thy importunacy?

PROTEUS
I likewise hear that Valentine is dead.

SILVIA
And so suppose am I; for in his grave   110
Assure thyself my love is burièd.

PROTEUS
Sweet lady, let me rake it from the earth.

SILVIA
Go to thy lady's grave and call hers thence;
Or, at the least, in hers sepulchre thine.

JULIA (*aside*)
He heard not that.

PROTEUS
Madam, if your heart be so obdurate,
Vouchsafe me yet your picture for my love,
The picture that is hanging in your chamber;
To that I'll speak, to that I'll sigh and weep;
For since the substance of your perfect self   120
Is else devoted, I am but a shadow;
And to your shadow will I make true love.

JULIA (*aside*)
If 'twere a substance, you would sure deceive it
And make it but a shadow, as I am.

SILVIA
I am very loath to be your idol, sir;
But, since your falsehood shall become you well
To worship shadows and adore false shapes,
Send to me in the morning and I'll send it;
And so, good rest.

PROTEUS   As wretches have o'ernight
That wait for execution in the morn.   130

Exeunt Proteus and Silvia

JULIA Host, will you go?

HOST By my halidom, I was fast asleep.

JULIA Pray you, where lies Sir Proteus?

HOST Marry, at my house. Trust me, I think 'tis almost day.

JULIA
　Not so; but it hath been the longest night
　That e'er I watched, and the most heaviest.　　*Exeunt*

IV.3　　　*Enter Eglamour*

EGLAMOUR
　This is the hour that Madam Silvia
　Entreated me to call and know her mind;
　There's some great matter she'd employ me in.
　Madam, madam!
　　　Enter Silvia at an upstairs window

SILVIA　　　　　　Who calls?

EGLAMOUR　　　　　　　Your servant and your friend;
　One that attends your ladyship's command.

SILVIA
　Sir Eglamour, a thousand times good morrow.

EGLAMOUR
　As many, worthy lady, to yourself!
　According to your ladyship's impose,
　I am thus early come, to know what service
10　It is your pleasure to command me in.

SILVIA
　O Eglamour, thou art a gentleman –
　Think not I flatter, for I swear I do not –
　Valiant, wise, remorseful, well-accomplished.
　Thou art not ignorant what dear good will
　I bear unto the banished Valentine;
　Nor how my father would enforce me marry
　Vain Thurio, whom my very soul abhors.

Thyself hast loved, and I have heard thee say
No grief did ever come so near thy heart
As when thy lady and thy true love died, 20
Upon whose grave thou vowedst pure chastity.
Sir Eglamour, I would to Valentine,
To Mantua, where I hear he makes abode;
And, for the ways are dangerous to pass,
I do desire thy worthy company,
Upon whose faith and honour I repose.
Urge not my father's anger, Eglamour,
But think upon my grief, a lady's grief,
And on the justice of my flying hence,
To keep me from a most unholy match, 30
Which heaven and fortune still rewards with plagues.
I do desire thee, even from a heart
As full of sorrows as the sea of sands,
To bear me company and go with me;
If not, to hide what I have said to thee,
That I may venture to depart alone.

EGLAMOUR
Madam, I pity much your grievances;
Which since I know they virtuously are placed,
I give consent to go along with you,
Recking as little what betideth me 40
As much I wish all good befortune you.
When will you go?

SILVIA   This evening coming.

EGLAMOUR
Where shall I meet you?

SILVIA   At Friar Patrick's cell,
Where I intend holy confession.

EGLAMOUR I will not fail your ladyship. Good morrow,
gentle lady.

SILVIA Good morrow, kind Sir Eglamour. *Exeunt*

LAUNCE When a man's servant shall play the cur with
him, look you, it goes hard – one that I brought up of a
puppy; one that I saved from drowning, when three or
four of his blind brothers and sisters went to it. I have
taught him, even as one would say precisely, 'Thus I
would teach a dog.' I was sent to deliver him as a present
to Mistress Silvia from my master; and I came no sooner
into the dining-chamber, but he steps me to her
trencher and steals her capon's leg. O, 'tis a foul thing
when a cur cannot keep himself in all companies! I
would have, as one should say, one that takes upon him
to be a dog indeed, to be, as it were, a dog at all things.
If I had not had more wit than he, to take a fault upon
me that he did, I think verily he had been hanged for't;
sure as I live, he had suffered for't. You shall judge. He
thrusts me himself into the company of three or four
gentlemanlike dogs under the Duke's table; he had not
been there, bless the mark, a pissing while but all the
chamber smelt him. 'Out with the dog!' says one;
'What cur is that?' says another; 'Whip him out,' says
the third; 'Hang him up,' says the Duke. I, having been
acquainted with the smell before, knew it was Crab, and
goes me to the fellow that whips the dogs. 'Friend,'
quoth I, 'you mean to whip the dog?' 'Ay, marry, do I,'
quoth he. 'You do him the more wrong,' quoth I,
''twas I did the thing you wot of.' He makes me no
more ado, but whips me out of the chamber. How many
masters would do this for his servant? Nay, I'll be
sworn, I have sat in the stocks for puddings he hath
stolen, otherwise he had been executed; I have stood on
the pillory for geese he hath killed, otherwise he had
suffered for't. Thou thinkest not of this now. Nay, I
remember the trick you served me when I took my leave

of Madam Silvia. Did not I bid thee still mark me and
do as I do? When didst thou see me heave up my leg
and make water against a gentlewoman's farthingale?
Didst thou ever see me do such a trick?

Enter Proteus, and Julia in a page's costume

PROTEUS
Sebastian is thy name? I like thee well,
And will employ thee in some service presently.

JULIA
In what you please; I will do what I can.   40

PROTEUS
I hope thou wilt. (*To Launce*) How now, you whoreson
    peasant!
Where have you been these two days loitering?

LAUNCE Marry, sir, I carried Mistress Silvia the dog you
bade me.

PROTEUS And what says she to my little jewel?

LAUNCE Marry, she says your dog was a cur, and tells you
currish thanks is good enough for such a present.

PROTEUS But she received my dog?

LAUNCE No, indeed, did she not; here have I brought
him back again.   50

PROTEUS What, didst thou offer her this from me?

LAUNCE Ay, sir; the other squirrel was stolen from me by
the hangman boys in the market-place; and then I
offered her mine own, who is a dog as big as ten of
yours, and therefore the gift the greater.

PROTEUS
Go get thee hence and find my dog again,
Or ne'er return again into my sight.
Away, I say! Stayest thou to vex me here?

Exit Launce

A slave that still an end turns me to shame!
Sebastian, I have entertainèd thee,   60

Partly that I have need of such a youth
That can with some discretion do my business,
For 'tis no trusting to yond foolish lout;
But chiefly for thy face and thy behaviour,
Which, if my augury deceive me not,
Witness good bringing up, fortune, and truth;
Therefore, know thou, for this I entertain thee.
Go presently, and take this ring with thee,
Deliver it to Madam Silvia –

70 She loved me well delivered it to me.

JULIA

It seems you loved not her, to leave her token.
She is dead, belike?

PROTEUS   Not so; I think she lives.

JULIA

Alas!

PROTEUS

Why dost thou cry 'Alas'?

JULIA   I cannot choose
But pity her.

PROTEUS   Wherefore shouldst thou pity her?

JULIA

Because methinks that she loved you as well
As you do love your lady Silvia.
She dreams on him that has forgot her love;
You dote on her that cares not for your love;

80 'Tis pity love should be so contrary;
And thinking on it makes me cry 'Alas!'

PROTEUS

Well, give her that ring, and therewithal
This letter. That's her chamber. Tell my lady
I claim the promise for her heavenly picture.
Your message done, hie home unto my chamber,
Where thou shalt find me sad and solitary.   *Exit*

JULIA

  How many women would do such a message?
  Alas, poor Proteus, thou hast entertained
  A fox to be the shepherd of thy lambs.
  Alas, poor fool, why do I pity him   90
  That with his very heart despiseth me?
  Because he loves her, he despiseth me;
  Because I love him, I must pity him.
  This ring I gave him, when he parted from me,
  To bind him to remember my good will;
  And now am I, unhappy messenger,
  To plead for that which I would not obtain,
  To carry that which I would have refused,
  To praise his faith, which I would have dispraised.
  I am my master's true confirmèd love,   100
  But cannot be true servant to my master,
  Unless I prove false traitor to myself.
  Yet will I woo for him, but yet so coldly
  As, heaven it knows, I would not have him speed.
      Enter Silvia with Attendants
  Gentlewoman, good day! I pray you, be my mean
  To bring me where to speak with Madam Silvia.

SILVIA

  What would you with her, if that I be she?

JULIA

  If you be she, I do entreat your patience
  To hear me speak the message I am sent on.

SILVIA

  From whom?   110

JULIA

  From my master, Sir Proteus, madam.

SILVIA

  O, he sends you for a picture.

JULIA

Ay, madam.

SILVIA

Ursula, bring my picture there.

> *Exit one of the Attendants. She returns with a portrait of Silvia*

Go, give your master this. Tell him from me,
One Julia, that his changing thoughts forget,
Would better fit his chamber than this shadow.

JULIA

Madam, please you peruse this letter –
Pardon me, madam; I have unadvised
120 Delivered you a paper that I should not.

> *Julia takes back the letter she offers and gives Silvia another one*

This is the letter to your ladyship.

SILVIA

I pray thee let me look on that again.

JULIA

It may not be; good madam, pardon me.

SILVIA

There, hold!

> *She tears the letter*

I will not look upon your master's lines.
I know they are stuffed with protestations,
And full of new-found oaths, which he will break
As easily as I do tear his paper.

JULIA

Madam, he sends your ladyship this ring.

SILVIA

130 The more shame for him that he sends it me;
For I have heard him say a thousand times
His Julia gave it him, at his departure.
Though his false finger have profaned the ring,

Mine shall not do his Julia so much wrong.

JULIA
She thanks you.

SILVIA
What sayest thou?

JULIA
I thank you, madam, that you tender her.
Poor gentlewoman! My master wrongs her much.

SILVIA
Dost thou know her?

JULIA
Almost as well as I do know myself. 140
To think upon her woes, I do protest
That I have wept a hundred several times.

SILVIA
Belike she thinks that Proteus hath forsook her.

JULIA
I think she doth, and that's her cause of sorrow.

SILVIA
Is she not passing fair?

JULIA
She hath been fairer, madam, than she is.
When she did think my master loved her well,
She, in my judgement, was as fair as you;
But since she did neglect her looking-glass
And threw her sun-expelling mask away, 150
That air hath starved the roses in her cheeks
And pinched the lily-tincture of her face,
That now she is become as black as I.

SILVIA
How tall was she?

JULIA
About my stature; for, at Pentecost,
When all our pageants of delight were played,

Our youth got me to play the woman's part
And I was trimmed in Madam Julia's gown,
Which servèd me as fit, by all men's judgements,
160 As if the garment had been made for me;
Therefore I know she is about my height.
And at that time I made her weep agood,
For I did play a lamentable part.
Madam, 'twas Ariadne passioning
For Theseus' perjury and unjust flight;
Which I so lively acted with my tears
That my poor mistress, movèd therewithal,
Wept bitterly; and would I might be dead
If I in thought felt not her very sorrow.

SILVIA

170 She is beholding to thee, gentle youth.
Alas, poor lady, desolate and left!
I weep myself, to think upon thy words.
Here, youth; there is my purse; I give thee this
For thy sweet mistress' sake, because thou lovest her.
Farewell.

Exeunt Silvia and attendants

JULIA

And she shall thank you for't, if e'er you know her.
A virtuous gentlewoman, mild, and beautiful!
I hope my master's suit will be but cold,
Since she respects my mistress' love so much.
180 Alas, how love can trifle with itself!
Here is her picture; let me see. I think
If I had such a tire this face of mine
Were full as lovely as is this of hers;
And yet the painter flattered her a little,
Unless I flatter with myself too much.
Her hair is auburn, mine is perfect yellow;
If that be all the difference in his love,

I'll get me such a coloured periwig.
Her eyes are grey as glass, and so are mine;
Ay, but her forehead's low, and mine's as high.   190
What should it be that he respects in her
But I can make respective in myself,
If this fond Love were not a blinded god?
Come, shadow, come, and take this shadow up,
For 'tis thy rival. O, thou senseless form,
Thou shalt be worshipped, kissed, loved, and adored!
And were there sense in his idolatry,
My substance should be statue in thy stead.
I'll use thee kindly for thy mistress' sake,
That used me so; or else, by Jove I vow,   200
I should have scratched out your unseeing eyes,
To make my master out of love with thee!   *Exit*

✳

Enter Eglamour   V.1

EGLAMOUR

The sun begins to gild the western sky,
And now it is about the very hour
That Silvia at Friar Patrick's cell should meet me.
She will not fail, for lovers break not hours
Unless it be to come before their time,
So much they spur their expedition.

    Enter Silvia

See where she comes. Lady, a happy evening!

SILVIA

Amen, amen! Go on, good Eglamour,
Out at the postern by the abbey wall;
I fear I am attended by some spies.

EGLAMOUR

> Fear not. The forest is not three leagues off;
> If we recover that, we are sure enough. *Exeunt*

V.2   *Enter Thurio, Proteus, and Julia dressed in a page's*
            costume

THURIO

> Sir Proteus, what says Silvia to my suit?

PROTEUS

> O, sir, I find her milder than she was;
> And yet she takes exceptions at your person.

THURIO

> What? That my leg is too long?

PROTEUS

> No, that it is too little.

THURIO

> I'll wear a boot to make it somewhat rounder.

JULIA (*aside*)

> But love will not be spurred to what it loathes.

THURIO

> What says she to my face?

PROTEUS

> She says it is a fair one.

THURIO

10   Nay then, the wanton lies; my face is black.

PROTEUS

> But pearls are fair; and the old saying is:
> Black men are pearls in beauteous ladies' eyes.

JULIA (*aside*)

> 'Tis true, such pearls as put out ladies' eyes;
> For I had rather wink than look on them.

THURIO

> How likes she my discourse?

126

PROTEUS

Ill, when you talk of war.

THURIO

But well when I discourse of love and peace.

JULIA (*aside*)

But better, indeed, when you hold your peace.

THURIO

What says she to my valour?

PROTEUS

O, sir, she makes no doubt of that.   20

JULIA (*aside*)

She needs not, when she knows it cowardice.

THURIO

What says she to my birth?

PROTEUS

That you are well derived.

JULIA (*aside*)

True; from a gentleman to a fool.

THURIO

Considers she my possessions?

PROTEUS

O, ay; and pities them.

THURIO

Wherefore?

JULIA (*aside*)

That such an ass should owe them.

PROTEUS

That they are out by lease.
      Enter the Duke of Milan

JULIA

Here comes the Duke.   30

DUKE

How now, Sir Proteus! How now, Thurio!
Which of you saw Sir Eglamour of late?

THURIO

Not I.

PROTEUS Nor I.

DUKE Saw you my daughter?

PROTEUS Neither.

DUKE

Why then,

She's fled unto that peasant Valentine;

And Eglamour is in her company.

'Tis true; for Friar Laurence met them both

As he in penance wandered through the forest;

Him he knew well, and guessed that it was she,

40 But, being masked, he was not sure of it;

Besides, she did intend confession

At Patrick's cell this even; and there she was not.

These likelihoods confirm her flight from hence;

Therefore, I pray you, stand not to discourse,

But mount you presently, and meet with me

Upon the rising of the mountain-foot

That leads toward Mantua, whither they are fled.

Dispatch, sweet gentlemen, and follow me. *Exit*

THURIO

Why, this it is to be a peevish girl

50 That flies her fortune when it follows her.

I'll after, more to be revenged on Eglamour

Than for the love of reckless Silvia. *Exit*

PROTEUS

And I will follow, more for Silvia's love

Than hate of Eglamour, that goes with her. *Exit*

JULIA

And I will follow, more to cross that love

Than hate for Silvia, that is gone for love. *Exit*

FIRST OUTLAW

  Come, come,
  Be patient; we must bring you to our captain.

SILVIA

  A thousand more mischances than this one
  Have learned me how to brook this patiently.

SECOND OUTLAW

  Come, bring her away.

FIRST OUTLAW

  Where is the gentleman that was with her?

THIRD OUTLAW

  Being nimble-footed, he hath outrun us,
  But Moyses and Valerius follow him.
  Go thou with her to the west end of the wood;
  There is our captain; we'll follow him that's fled.   10
  The thicket is beset; he cannot 'scape.

FIRST OUTLAW

  Come, I must bring you to our captain's cave;
  Fear not; he bears an honourable mind,
  And will not use a woman lawlessly.

SILVIA

  O Valentine, this I endure for thee!   *Exeunt*

  Enter Valentine   V.4

VALENTINE

  How use doth breed a habit in a man!
  This shadowy desert, unfrequented woods,
  I better brook than flourishing peopled towns.
  Here can I sit alone, unseen of any,
  And to the nightingale's complaining notes
  Tune my distresses, and record my woes.
  O thou that dost inhabit in my breast,

Leave not the mansion so long tenantless,
Lest, growing ruinous, the building fall
10 And leave no memory of what it was!
Repair me with thy presence, Silvia;
Thou gentle nymph, cherish thy forlorn swain.
  Noises within
What halloing and what stir is this today?
These are my mates, that make their wills their law,
Have some unhappy passenger in chase.
They love me well; yet I have much to do
To keep them from uncivil outrages.
Withdraw thee, Valentine. Who's this comes here?
  He steps aside
  Enter Proteus, Silvia, and Julia in a page's costume

PROTEUS
Madam, this service I have done for you,
20 Though you respect not aught your servant doth,
To hazard life, and rescue you from him
That would have forced your honour and your love.
Vouchsafe me, for my meed, but one fair look;
A smaller boon than this I cannot beg,
And less than this, I am sure, you cannot give.

VALENTINE (*aside*)
How like a dream is this I see and hear!
Love, lend me patience to forbear awhile.

SILVIA
O miserable, unhappy that I am!

PROTEUS
Unhappy were you, madam, ere I came;
30 But by my coming I have made you happy.

SILVIA
By thy approach thou makest me most unhappy.

JULIA (*aside*)
And me, when he approacheth to your presence.

SILVIA

    Had I been seizèd by a hungry lion,
    I would have been a breakfast to the beast,
    Rather than have false Proteus rescue me.
    O, heaven be judge how I love Valentine,
    Whose life's as tender to me as my soul!
    And full as much, for more there cannot be,
    I do detest false perjured Proteus.
    Therefore be gone; solicit me no more.   40

PROTEUS

    What dangerous action, stood it next to death,
    Would I not undergo for one calm look?
    O, 'tis the curse in love, and still approved,
    When women cannot love where they're beloved!

SILVIA

    When Proteus cannot love where he's beloved!
    Read over Julia's heart, thy first best love,
    For whose dear sake thou didst then rend thy faith
    Into a thousand oaths; and all those oaths
    Descended into perjury, to love me.
    Thou hast no faith left now, unless thou'dst two,   50
    And that's far worse than none; better have none
    Than plural faith, which is too much by one.
    Thou counterfeit to thy true friend!

PROTEUS   In love,

    Who respects friend?

SILVIA   All men but Proteus.

PROTEUS

    Nay, if the gentle spirit of moving words
    Can no way change you to a milder form,
    I'll woo you like a soldier, at arms' end,
    And love you 'gainst the nature of love – force ye.

SILVIA

    O heaven!

PROTEUS   I'll force thee yield to my desire.
Valentine steps forward

VALENTINE
60   Ruffian, let go that rude uncivil touch;
Thou friend of an ill fashion!

PROTEUS   Valentine!

VALENTINE
Thou common friend that's without faith or love –
For such is a friend now; treacherous man,
Thou hast beguiled my hopes; naught but mine eye
Could have persuaded me. Now I dare not say
I have one friend alive: thou wouldst disprove me.
Who should be trusted now, when one's right hand
Is perjured to the bosom? Proteus,
I am sorry I must never trust thee more,
70   But count the world a stranger for thy sake.
The private wound is deepest. O time most accurst!
'Mongst all foes that a friend should be the worst!

PROTEUS
My shame and guilt confounds me.
Forgive me, Valentine; if hearty sorrow
Be a sufficient ransom for offence,
I tender't here; I do as truly suffer
As e'er I did commit.

VALENTINE   Then I am paid;
And once again I do receive thee honest.
Who by repentance is not satisfied
80   Is nor of heaven nor earth, for these are pleased;
By penitence th'Eternal's wrath's appeased.
And, that my love may appear plain and free,
All that was mine in Silvia I give thee.

JULIA O me unhappy!
She swoons

PROTEUS Look to the boy.

VALENTINE Why, boy? Why, wag, how now? What's the matter? Look up; speak.

JULIA O, good sir, my master charged me to deliver a ring to Madam Silvia, which, out of my neglect, was never done. 90

PROTEUS Where is that ring, boy?

JULIA Here 'tis; this is it.

She offers her own ring

PROTEUS How? Let me see. Why, this is the ring I gave to Julia.

JULIA
O, cry you mercy, sir, I have mistook;
This is the ring you sent to Silvia.

She offers another ring

PROTEUS But how camest thou by this ring? At my depart I gave this unto Julia.

JULIA
And Julia herself did give it me;
And Julia herself hath brought it hither. 100

PROTEUS
How? Julia?

JULIA
Behold her that gave aim to all thy oaths,
And entertained 'em deeply in her heart.
How oft hast thou with perjury cleft the root!
O Proteus, let this habit make thee blush!
Be thou ashamed that I have took upon me
Such an immodest raiment, if shame live
In a disguise of love.
It is the lesser blot, modesty finds,
Women to change their shapes than men their minds. 110

PROTEUS
Than men their minds? 'Tis true. O heaven, were man
But constant, he were perfect! That one error

Fills him with faults; makes him run through all the
     sins:
Inconstancy falls off ere it begins.
What is in Silvia's face, but I may spy
More fresh in Julia's with a constant eye?

VALENTINE
Come, come, a hand from either.
Let me be blest to make this happy close;
'Twere pity two such friends should be long foes.

PROTEUS
120 Bear witness, heaven, I have my wish for ever.

JULIA
And I mine.
    Enter the Outlaws, with the Duke of Milan and
    Thurio captives

OUTLAWS
A prize, a prize, a prize!

VALENTINE   Forbear,
Forbear, I say! It is my lord the Duke.
Your grace is welcome to a man disgraced,
Banishèd Valentine.

DUKE   Sir Valentine?

THURIO
Yonder is Silvia; and Silvia's mine.

VALENTINE
Thurio, give back, or else embrace thy death;
Come not within the measure of my wrath;
Do not name Silvia thine; if once again,
130 Verona shall not hold thee. Here she stands;
Take but possession of her with a touch –
I dare thee but to breathe upon my love.

THURIO
Sir Valentine, I care not for her, I:

I hold him but a fool that will endanger
His body for a girl that loves him not.
I claim her not and therefore she is thine.

DUKE

The more degenerate and base art thou
To make such means for her as thou hast done,
And leave her on such slight conditions.
Now, by the honour of my ancestry,   140
I do applaud thy spirit, Valentine,
And think thee worthy of an empress' love.
Know, then, I here forget all former griefs,
Cancel all grudge, repeal thee home again,
Plead a new state in thy unrivalled merit,
To which I thus subscribe: Sir Valentine.
Thou art a gentleman, and well derived;
Take thou thy Silvia, for thou hast deserved her.

VALENTINE

I thank your grace; the gift hath made me happy.
I now beseech you, for your daughter's sake,   150
To grant one boon that I shall ask of you.

DUKE

I grant it, for thine own, whate'er it be.

VALENTINE

These banished men, that I have kept withal,
Are men endued with worthy qualities;
Forgive them what they have committed here,
And let them be recalled from their exile:
They are reformèd, civil, full of good,
And fit for great employment, worthy lord.

DUKE

Thou hast prevailed; I pardon them and thee;
Dispose of them as thou knowest their deserts.   160
Come, let us go; we will include all jars

135

With triumphs, mirth, and rare solemnity.

VALENTINE

And, as we walk along, I dare be bold
With our discourse to make your grace to smile.
What think you of this page, my lord?

DUKE

I think the boy hath grace in him; he blushes.

VALENTINE

I warrant you, my lord – more grace than boy.

DUKE

What mean you by that saying?

VALENTINE

Please you, I'll tell you as we pass along,
170 That you will wonder what hath fortunèd.
Come, Proteus, 'tis your penance but to hear
The story of your loves discoverèd.
That done, our day of marriage shall be yours:
One feast, one house, one mutual happiness.   *Exeunt*

COMMENTARY

THE act and scene divisions are those of the Folio (F). All references to plays by Shakespeare not yet published in the New Penguin Shakespeare are to Peter Alexander's edition of the *Complete Works* (London, 1951). Passages from Jorge de Montemayor's *La Diana* (translated by B. Yong in 1598) are modern-spelling versions of the text, found, under the title 'The Story of Felix and Felismena', in *Elizabethan Love Stories*, edited by T. J. B. Spencer (1968); those from Sir Thomas Elyot's *Book of the Governor* (1531) are modern-spelling versions of the text, found in *Narrative and Dramatic Sources of Shakespeare*, edited by G. Bullough, Volume I, (1957); page references are given to these sources. Quotations from the works of John Lyly are modern-spelling versions of the text, found in R. W. Bond's edition of *The Complete Works of John Lyly* (1902), to which references are given.

1.1   (stage direction) *Valentine*. By association with the St Valentine's Day tradition the word means 'a true lover'. See Launce's and Valentine's quibbles on the name at III.1.191–214.

         Proteus. The name is spelt *Protheus* throughout the F text. In Greek mythology Proteus was an old man of the sea who guarded the flocks of Poseidon. Although he had the gift of prophecy, those who wished to consult him found that on being questioned he eluded them by assuming different shapes.

2   *Home-keeping youth have ever homely wits.* Among the upper classes of Shakespeare's day travelling was beginning to be considered an educational and broadening experience appropriate for a young man.

Compare Lucentio's attitude in *The Taming of the Shrew* (I.1.1–24), and Petruchio's conversation with Hortensio at I.2.47–51 in the same play:

HORTENSIO

   And tell me now, sweet friend, what happy gale
   Blows you to Padua here from old Verona?

PETRUCHIO

   Such wind as scatters young men through the world
   To seek their fortunes farther than at home,
   Where small experience grows.

3   *affection* passion, love

8   *shapeless* aimless, without guidance or direction

9   *still* always, constantly

12–13   *Think on thy Proteus, when thou haply seest | Some rare noteworthy object in thy travel.* This is ironical in view of the fact that Silvia is to be the most *rare noteworthy object* that Valentine is to meet in Milan.

12   *haply* by chance

15   *hap* fortune

18   *beadsman.* This was a holy man engaged to pray (that is, tell the beads of his rosary) for another person.

19   *love-book* (manual of courtship or a romance, instead of a prayer-book)

21   *shallow story of deep love.* The quibble here is on *shallow* and *deep* water and *shallow* (not profound) and *deep* (passionate) love.

22   *How young Leander crossed the Hellespont.* The reference is to the legend of Leander who swam the Hellespont each night to visit his mistress, Hero. It may also be an allusion to Christopher Marlowe's poem *Hero and Leander*, which was entered for publication in the Register of the Stationers' Company in 1593, after Marlowe's death, but was not printed until 1598.

23   *deep story of a deeper love.* The quibble is on *deep* (meaning 'profound', 'tragic') and *deeper* (meaning 'farther in the depths of the sea'), the allusion being

to Leander's ultimate death by drowning as he crossed the Hellespont in rough weather.

24   *over-shoes in love* determined recklessly to pursue his love affair. The quibble is with *over-shoes* (meaning 'wet above the shoes') as Leander was in the Hellespont.

25   *over-boots.* This has the same meaning as *over-shoes*; see note to line 24.

27   *give me not the boots.* This is a proverbial expression meaning 'do not make a fool of me, do not play with me'.

28   *it boots thee not* it avails you not. The quibble is with the proverbial phrase in line 27.

29–35   *To be in love, where scorn is bought with groans ... vanquishèd.* This passage is made up of Renaissance commonplaces about romantic love and contains most of the conventional attitudes attributed to the lover at this period. Compare Speed's satirical picture of the lover at II.1.17–30. More specifically the tone of the passage, as well as the play's opposition between love and friendship, recalls John Lyly's *Euphues, The Anatomy of Wit*, an enormously popular and influential novel published in 1578.

32–3   *If haply won, perhaps a hapless gain; | If lost, why then a grievous labour won.* These lines are sometimes taken as an allusion to Shakespeare's play *Love's Labour's Lost* and to the play *Love's Labour's Won*, which is not extant but which is listed as being by Shakespeare in Francis Meres's *Palladis Tamia* (1598).

32   *haply* by chance
       hapless unfortunate

34   *However* in any case, however it may turn out

34–5   *a folly bought with wit, | Or else a wit by folly vanquishèd.* This was an Elizabethan commonplace; compare *As You Like It* (II.7.182): 'Most friendship is feigning, most loving mere folly.'

34   *wit* intellect, mind

36   *circumstance* peroration, argument, detailed discourse

37   *circumstance* situation, condition

41   *chronicled for wise*. Literally this means 'set down in
        the Chronicle for wisdom', but here it merely means
        'reputed to be wise'.

43   *canker* cankerworm

44   *Inhabits in* dwells in
        wits minds, intellects

45   *forward* advanced in growth

46   *blow* bloom, blossom

49   *his verdure* its fresh or flourishing condition
        prime spring

50   *fair effects of future hopes* prosperous fulfilment of
        future happiness

52   *votary to* addicted to (with the religious overtone
        implying 'worshipping')
        fond doting (and thus 'foolish')

53   *road* harbour, anchorage

54   *shipped*. Both Valentine here and Proteus (at II.2.14
        and II.4.185) go by sea from Verona to Milan;
        whereas Julia makes the journey overland (see
        II.7.8–10, 35), as does Valentine on his return
        journey. One of the features of the F text is the con-
        fusion in place names and locations; see An Account
        of the Text, page 203.

55   *bring* accompany

57   *To Milan*. Although some editors emend with F2 to
        At Milan, the syntax is not unusual and means 'by
        letters (sent) to Milan'.

58   *success* fortune (good or bad)

59   *Betideth* takes place

61   *bechance* befall

65   *leave*. The F reading *love* makes no sense here and is
        probably a compositor's misreading of 'loue' for
        'leue'.

66–9 *Thou, Julia, thou hast metamorphosed me ... with*

thought. Proteus describes here all the symptoms generally ascribed to the young lover during the Elizabethan period; compare *Romeo and Juliet*, I.1.171–237.

66   *metamorphosed*. This is the first reference in the play to the traditional Protean nature.

67   *lose* waste

69   *thought* brooding melancholy

70   *save you* God save you (a common greeting of the time)

73   *sheep*. This is a quibble on 'ship' (from *shipped* in line 72), the two words being apparently pronounced sufficiently alike at the time. Compare the similar use in *The Comedy of Errors* (IV.1.91) and *Love's Labour's Lost* (II.1.218).

75   *An* if. 'An if' was a frequently used double form.

79   *my horns are his horns*. It has been suggested that the reference here is to the rhyme 'Little Boy Blue'; but it is possibly a pointless allusion to the horns of the cuckold.

84   *circumstance* detailed proof or argument

93   '*baa*'. The quibble is with 'bah!'.

94–5   *Gavest thou my letter to Julia?* There is no reason why Proteus should employ Valentine's servant rather than Launce, except possibly for secrecy in his affair which at I.3.51–9 he seems intent on keeping from his father's knowledge. In *La Diana*, Don Felix (Proteus) also makes his first approach to his mistress by means of a letter which is conveyed to Felismena (Julia) by her maid Rosina (Lucetta); see *Elizabethan Love Stories*, pages 132–3.

96–7   *I, a lost mutton, gave your letter to her, a laced mutton.* It is clear, however, from the exchange between Julia and Lucetta at I.2.34 ff. that Speed did not meet Julia, so that here he has been talking about the maid's rather than the mistress's behaviour.

97   *laced mutton*. This was a cant term for a prostitute,

with *laced* referring either to the lace or slashing of
her dress or to her tight lacing. Speed pronounced
laced sufficiently like *lost* to pun with his phrase in
line 96. The way in which Proteus accepts this
impertinence has caused many editors to suspect that
this exchange is an interpolation. However, there is
ample evidence in Shakespeare's other plays to indicate that the relationship between young men and
their servants was a good deal more flexible than
class-conscious nineteenth-century commentators
are prepared to allow. Good-humoured familiarity
between the young master and his servant was also
a feature of the Roman comedies of Plautus and
Terence, which Shakespeare knew well.

101   *overcharged* overburdened, overstocked (with sheep)
        you were best it would be best for you
        stick stab, slaughter (the excessive sheep). Speed
        almost certainly means to suggest a bawdy quibble
        (the mutton meaning the prostitute).

103   *astray*. Proteus is echoing Speed's phrase *I, a lost
        mutton* and quibbles 'a stray'.
        pound. The quibble is on the two meanings 'enclose'
        (like a stray sheep) and 'beat'.

105   *pound*. Speed deliberately misunderstands Proteus,
        and assumes he is referring to the sum of money
        Speed will be paid for the errand.

107   *pinfold* enclosure for stray animals

108–9   *From a pound to a pin? Fold it over and over,* | *'Tis
        threefold too little for carrying a letter to your lover.*
        F prints these lines as rhyming doggerel; and they
        could be delivered as bad impromptu verse in the
        theatre.

108   *a pin* (something of no value)

110–13 PROTEUS *But what said she?* Speed nods *A nod?*
        SPEED *Ay.* PROTEUS *Nod-ay? Why, that's noddy.*
        Most editors have felt it necessary to emend the F
        version of this passage so as to make the action con-

form to Speed's description in lines 114–15. See Collations 2 for other emendations which have been suggested.

113   *noddy* simpleton
120   *fain* pleased
      bear with you. The quibble is on the two meanings: 'endure' and 'support'.
122   *Marry*. This was a common exclamation meaning originally 'by the Virgin Mary'.
      nothing. The pun is with 'nodding' (through previous use of *nod* and *noddy*).
124   *Beshrew me* (a mild oath used for emphasis)
126   *open* disclose
129   *delivered*. Speed is playing on the two meanings: '(the money) handed over' and '(the account) reported'.
133   *perceive* receive
136   *ducat* (a gold or silver coin)
138   *in telling your mind* when you tell her in person
139   *stones*. The reference may be to diamonds which would be a suitable gift for someone with a hard nature.
142   *testerned* tipped with a tester (or sixpence). This coin was worth about one seventh of the ducat that Speed mentions hopefully in line 136.
147   *destined to a drier death on shore*. The reference is to the proverb 'He that is born to be hanged shall never be drowned'.
149–50   *I fear my Julia would not deign my lines, | Receiving them from such a worthless post*. This emphasis on appearance is characteristic of Proteus's way of thinking and quite different from Julia's. See Introduction, pages 16–17.
149   *deign* condescend to accept, take graciously
150   *post*. The two meanings suggested are 'messenger' and 'door-post' (that is, blockhead).

I.2.1–33   *But say, Lucetta, now we are alone ... his mind.*
            Shakespeare was to use this situation with greater wit
            in *The Merchant of Venice*, I.2, where Portia and
            Nerissa discuss the suitors at Belmont. In *La Diana*
            Felismena (Julia) relates how her maid Rosina
            (Lucetta) delivered the letter to her: 'But to see
            the means that Rosina made unto me ... the duti-
            ful services and unwonted circumstances before
            she did deliver it, the oaths that she sware unto me,
            and the subtle words and serious protestations she
            used, it was a pleasant thing and worthy the noting'
            (*Elizabethan Love Stories*, page 133).

4   *resort* company, gathering

5   *parle* talk, conversation

6   *worthiest love* most worthy of love

7   *show my mind* give you a description of them as I see
            them

9   *Sir Eglamour.* The name appears to have been a type
            name for a carpet-knight. This is presumably a dif-
            ferent character from the Eglamour who accompanies
            Silvia on her flight in V.1, although her description in
            IV.3.11–13 is similar to Lucetta's here. The fact that
            the same name is used twice is another sign of the
            carelessness which characterizes the text.

10   *neat* refined, elegant

12   *Mercatio.* Some editors emend this to the commoner
            Italian form 'Mercutio' that Shakespeare uses in
            Romeo and Juliet.

17   *passing* surpassing

19   *censure* pass judgement

27   *moved me* approached me on the subject, made a
            proposal to me

30   *Fire that's closest kept burns most of all* (an Elizabethan
            proverb)
            Fire (pronounced with two syllables here)

33–40   *I would I knew his mind ... I pray.* The change in the
            metre occurs at the point where the subject of the

letter is introduced. Some editors think Shakespeare intended line 38 to be a continuation of the three-stress pattern and print it as two lines.

41-7   *Now, by my modesty, a goodly broker! . . . my sight.* In *La Diana* Felismena (Julia) also describes how she feigns annoyance with Rosina (Lucetta) on the delivery of the letter: 'To whom, nevertheless, with an angry countenance I turned again, saying: "If I had not regard of mine own estate and what hereafter might be said, I would make this shameless face of thine be known ever after for a mark of an impudent and bold minion. But because it is the first time, let this suffice that I have said and give thee warning to take heed of the second"' (*Elizabethan Love Stories*, page 133).

41   *broker* pandar, go-between

50-65   *And yet I would I had o'erlooked the letter . . . folly past.* The episode in *La Diana* is quite close to these lines: 'And with this . . . taking her letter with her, she departed from me. This having passed thus, I began to imagine what might ensue thereof. And love, methought, did put a certain desire into my mind to see the letter, though modesty and shame forbade me to ask it of my maid, especially for the words that had passed between us' (*Elizabethan Love Stories*, page 133).

50   *o'erlooked* perused

52   *to a fault* to commit a fault

53   *What 'fool.* The F apostrophe would appear to indicate the omission of the indirect article.

55-6   *Since maids, in modesty, say no to that | Which they would have the profferer construe ay* (an Elizabethan proverb)

56   *construe.* This is accented on the first syllable.

58   *testy* fretful

59   *presently* immediately

62   *angerly* angrily

68   *kill* allay, satisfy, subdue

        stomach. The pun is on the two meanings: 'appetite'
        and 'anger'.

69   *maid*. There is probably a pun here with *meat* which
        was often pronounced 'mate'.

70–100 *What is't that you took up so gingerly? . . . papers lie.*
        This is very close to a passage in *La Diana* where
        Felismena (Julia) describes the episode with her
        maid: . . . 'the discreet and subtle Rosina came
        into my chamber to help me to make me ready; in
        doing whereof, of purpose she let the letter closely
        fall; which when I perceived: "What is that that fell
        down?" said I. "Let me see it." "It is nothing,
        mistress," said she. "Come, come, let me see it,"
        said I. "What! move me not, or else tell me what it
        is." "Good Lord, mistress," said she, "why will you
        see it? It is the letter I would have given you yester-
        day." "Nay, that it is not," said I, "wherefore show
        it me, that I may see if you lie or no." I had no sooner
        said so but she put it into my hands, saying: "God
        never give me good if it be any other thing." And
        although I knew it well indeed, yet I said: "What,
        this is not the same; for I know that well enough. But
        it is one of thy lover's letters. I will read it, to see in
        what need he standeth of thy favour"' (*Elizabethan
        Love Stories*, page 134).

77   *lie* deceive (making a quibble with *lie* meaning
        'remain' in line 76)

        concerns is of importance

80–96   *That I might sing it, madam, to a tune . . . unruly bass.*
        All the quibbles in this exchange are based on the
        musical terminology of the period. See the subsequent
        notes for the meanings of individual terms.

81   *note*. The quibble is on the two meanings: 'letter'
        and 'musical note'.

        set. The two meanings are 'write' (a letter) and 'set
        to music'.

82 *As little by.* Julia picks up the word *set* in line 81 and turns it to mean 'set as little (store) by'.
    toys trifles

83 *'Light o'love'.* This was a popular tune of the period, to which Shakespeare also refers in *Much Ado About Nothing*, III.4.39.

84 *It is too heavy for so light a tune.* It is too important or weighty in content for a tune which is trivial in having no 'burden'.

85 *burden.* The two meanings are: 'load' and 'musical refrain or figure repeated throughout the song in the bass'. There is also a bawdy allusion to 'a woman's burden'.

87 *I cannot reach so high.* The two meanings are: 'it is beyond the range of my singing voice' and 'Proteus is of too high a social rank for a servant like me'.

89 *tune.* The two meanings are: 'correct musical pitch' and 'mood, humour'.

91 *sharp.* In keeping with the word-play, Lucetta refers here (1) to the musical notation and (2) to some piece of stage business performed by Julia, such as a slap or pinch, to make Lucetta release the letter.

93 *flat.* The two meanings are: 'the musical notation' and 'downright in attitude'.

94 *descant.* The reference is both to musical variations and to the variations of mood passed through by Julia.

95 *wanteth* needs, lacks
    mean tenor. Lucetta obviously means Proteus here, and there is possibly a pun with 'man'.

96 *bass.* The two meanings are: 'bass part of a song' and 'base' or 'low' (conduct).

97 *bid the bass.* The phrase is from a game called 'Prisoner's Base' in which a member of one team challenges the members of an opposite team to pursue him, thus giving the prisoner at base a chance to escape. Lucetta sees herself and Julia as opposing

team members with Proteus as the prisoner at base.

98   *babble*. There may be a pun here with the word 'bauble' meaning the letter.

99   *a coil with protestation* a fuss over a declaration of love

102–3   *She makes it strange, but she would be best pleased | To be so angered with another letter*. This is clearly intended by Lucetta as an address to the audience. However, Julia's line 104 indicates that she overhears her maid's remark, and so many editors do not mark the speech as an aside.

102   *makes it strange* pretends a lack of interest, displays indifference

104   *Nay, would I were so angered with the same!* Some editors have transferred this line to Lucetta by stressing the *I*. However, it is clear that Julia is merely regretting that she has torn the letter.

106   *Injurious* unjust
    wasps (her fingers)

108   *several* separate

110   *As* thus

115   *throughly* thoroughly

116   *search* probe, cleanse (and thus 'cure'). Julia uses a medical term in keeping with the *wound* in line 115.

121   *ragged* rugged
    fearful, hanging. Some editors make this phrase a compound adjective. The reference is probably to the Tarpeian Rock from which traitors were cast in ancient Rome.

124   *forlorn*. The accent is on the first syllable.

126   *sith* since

131   *stays* waits

134   *respect* set value on, prize
    best to take it were best you take

135   *taken up* rebuked

136   *for* for fear of

137   *a month's mind* a strong inclination, a keen desire. Originally this was a mass said in memory of someone

a month after his death, but later it came to refer to the desire for various foodstuffs characteristic of women in the last month of pregnancy. The word *month* has two syllables here, and was often spelt 'moneth'.

139   *wink* close my eyes (to them)

I.3   (stage direction) *Panthino*. This is the commonest form of the name in the F text, although it is spelled *Panthion* at some points. However, the spelling *Panthino* in F at I.3.76 indicates that the 'Panthino' form is the correct one.

1   *sad* serious

2   *cloister*. This is not necessarily a cathedral or monastery cloister, as the word was used to describe a colonnaded structure attached to other buildings.

4–16   *He wondered that your lordship . . . in his youth.* This is an elaboration of the idea noted at I.1.2. The parallel passage in *La Diana* is: '. . . his father . . . sent him to the great Princess Augusta Caesarina's court, telling him it was not meet that a young gentleman, and of so noble a house as he was, should spend his youth idly at home, where nothing could be learned but examples of vice' (*Elizabethan Love Stories*, page 136).

5   *suffer* allow

6   *of slender reputation* inconsequential, unimportant

7   *Put forth* send abroad

12   *meet* fitted

13   *importune* urge. The accent is on the second syllable.

15   *impeachment* discredit, reproach

18   *hammering* pondering

23   *perfected*. The accent is on the first syllable.

24   *were I best* would it be best for me

27   *Emperor*. Elsewhere in the text and in the list of

characters in F he is called a duke. See An Account of
the Text, page 203.

30   *tilts and tournaments.* A tilt was a mock battle be-
tween two knights and a tournament was one between
two parties of knights. In *La Diana* Don Felix
(Proteus) makes manifest his love for Felismena
(Julia) 'by sundry signs, as by tilt and tourneys'
(*Elizabethan Love Stories*, page 132).

31   *discourse.* The accent is on the second syllable.

32   *be in eye* have the opportunity of witnessing

33   *Worthy* worthy of

42   *commend* commit

44   *in good time* (a phrase frequently used when a person
arrives opportunely)

      break with him broach the matter to him

47   *pawn* pledge

48   *applaud* approve of

53   *commendations* greetings, remembrances

58   *gracèd* honoured

60   *stand you affected* are you disposed

63   *sorted with* corresponding to, in agreement with

64   *Muse* wonder

69   *exhibition* allowance of money for maintenance

71   *Excuse it not* do not make excuses (to evade the decision)

      peremptory determined. The accent is on the first
syllable.

72   *provided* equipped

74   *Look what* whatever

75   *No more of stay* no more talk of preventing (your
departure)

81   *take exceptions* make objections

83   *excepted . . . against* objected . . . to

84   *resembleth.* This is pronounced here with four
syllables.

91   *it answers.* The F reading *it answer's* may indicate that
the sense intended was 'its answer is'.

II.1.2   *but one.* The quibble is with *on* in line 1. The two
words were often spelt the same and could pre-
sumably be pronounced similarly.

11   *still* always

13   *Go to* (an expression of annoyance)

17–30   *Marry, by these special marks . . . my master.* Speed
describes ironically most of the attitudes attributed
to the lover. See I.1.29–35. Compare *As You Like
It*, III.2.358–66.

18   *wreathe* fold

18–19   *like a malcontent.* Folded arms were a posture often
associated with the melancholy man.

19   *relish* sing, warble
like a robin-redbreast. There is no obvious reason why
this bird should be singled out for association with
a love-song. Perhaps the meaning intended is that
Valentine spends his time alone and disconsolate like
a robin in winter.

21   *ABC* (a primer or horn-book used for teaching
children to read)

21–2   *to weep, like a young wench that had buried her
grandam* (a common proverb of the time)

22   *grandam* grandmother

23   *takes diet* is dieting for health purposes
watch lie awake

24   *puling* whiningly
like a beggar at Hallowmas. All Saints' Day or All-
Hallows (1 November) was traditionally a feast on
which paupers received special alms.

26   *like one of the lions.* This has been taken variously as
an allusion to the lions kept at the Tower of London
or to the heraldic lions on the royal standard which
may have been displayed in theatres.

27   *presently* immediately

28   *want* lack
metamorphosed changed in shape. Proteus applies the
same word to himself at I.1.66.

29   *with* by

         that so that

32   *without* outside

33   *Without me?* in my absence?

34   *without* unless

35   *would* (would perceive them). Dr Johnson suggested the meaning 'would be so simple'.

         without. The two meanings implied are: 'lacking' and 'outside'.

37   *urinal* (a transparent glass container used by doctors in testing a patient's urine)

46   *hard-favoured* ugly

47   *Not so fair, boy, as well-favoured* (Silvia's beauty is surpassed by her charm of manner)

50   *well favoured* looked on with favour

52   *favour* charm, graciousness

53   *painted.* The reference is to cosmetics.

54   *out of all count* beyond calculation, boundless

57   *counts of* takes account of, esteems

58   *account of* appreciate

60   *deformed.* Speed's point is that the lover sees the appearance of the beloved falsely. Valentine takes the word to mean 'misshapen'.

67   *Love is blind.* The allusion is to blind Cupid and to the power of self-deception in the lover.

68   *lights* powers to see clearly

69   *going ungartered.* This was considered one of the signs of the lovesick man; compare *As You Like It*, III.2.363.

73   *to put on your hose.* Speed is indicating that Valentine is in a worse state than Proteus, for whereas Proteus had difficulty only with the gartering of his hose, Valentine has difficulty with the hose themselves. There have been many emendations proposed for this phrase (see Collations 2), all of which change the point being made.

77   *swinged* thrashed

79   *stand affected to* am in love with. See note to line 80.

80   *set* seated. Speed takes up the normal meaning of Valentine's *stand* in line 79. There is also a bawdy jest intended by Speed in that he takes *stand* also to mean 'a sexual erection' and suggests by *set* 'put down' which would thus make his master less love-sick.

86   *lamely* not scanned correctly, lacking the correct number of metrical feet

89   *motion* a puppet show (or, sometimes, a single puppet)

90   *Now will he interpret to her*. The puppeteer not only manipulated the dolls in the play but also provided a commentary which 'interpreted' the action.

93   *give ye* God give you

95   *servant*. This was one of the terms of the courtly love convention, and was applied to any man paying attentions to a lady who had not committed herself to choosing him as her lover.

102   *clerkly* in a scholarly fashion (or, perhaps, with good penmanship)

103   *came hardly off* was difficult to perform

107   *stead* benefit, assist

110   *period* full pause

112   *again* back

116   *quaintly* skilfully, with ingenuity

134   *reasoning* discussing, talking of

140   *by a figure* indirectly. The term is from rhetoric.

147–8   *perceive her earnest*. The quibble is on the two meanings: 'see that she was serious' and 'see the sum she paid to bind a bargain'.

152–3   *there an end* there is nothing more to say about the matter

160   *speak in print* speak precisely or exactly
in print I found it. The phrase is difficult to explain. The second *in print* should be some kind of pun on the first *in print* ('plainly'). Speed seems to be claiming that his doggerel fourteeners are a quotation

153

from some book or ballad, so possibly they should be printed as a quotation and many editors do this. However, they have not been traced.

161   *muse* ponder

162   *I have dined.* Valentine implies he has feasted on the sight of Silvia.

163–4   *the chameleon Love can feed on the air.* The belief that the chameleon existed like this was a common one. Love was often called a chameleon because of the changeability of lovers.

166   *be moved.* The quibble is on the two meanings: 'have compassion' and 'be persuaded to go (to dinner)'.

II.2   If Shakespeare did use *La Diana* as his source then this scene marks a departure from the story where Felix (Proteus) 'went away so pensive that his great grief would not suffer him' to inform Felismena (Julia) of his departure (*Elizabethan Love Stories*, page 136).

2   *where is* where there is

4   *turn not* are not inconstant, do not prove unfaithful

6–8   *Why, then, we'll make exchange; here, take you this . . . true constancy.* Although there is no witness present Proteus and Julia are going through the forms of the betrothal ceremony: the joining of hands and the sealing kiss.

9   *o'erslips* passes by unnoticed

14   *The tide is now* the tide is right for sailing. See the note to I.1.54.

    tide of tears flood of tears. Compare the parody of these words at II.3.31–51.

17   *Ay, so true love should do; it cannot speak.* This is ironical in view of Proteus's loquaciousness and subsequent unfaithfulness.

19   *I come.* The F text reads *I come, I come.* However, as it is obvious that a rhymed couplet is intended to end

the scene, I have assumed the F reading to be due to a simple error of repetition on the part of the compositor.

II.3	(stage direction) *with his dog, Crab*. Dogs were not frequently used as actors on the Elizabethan stage although there are other examples of scenes requiring them.
1-30	*Nay, 'twill be this hour . . . with my tears*. For the dramatic relevance of this monologue to II.2 and to the love plot in general, see Introduction, pages 31-2.
2	*kind* family, kindred
	this very exactly this
3	*proportion* (a malapropism for 'portion')
	prodigious (a malapropism for 'prodigal')
4	*Imperial's* Emperor's. See note to I.3.27.
5	*sourest-natured*. The reference is to the dog's name *Crab* (meaning 'crab-apple').
12	*grandam* grandmother
13	*parting* departure
16	*the worser sole*. The reference is to the common medieval debate as to whether a woman's soul was inferior to a man's.
	sole. The quibble is on 'sole of the shoe' and 'soul'.
17	*This shoe with the hole in it*. Thus, the *worser sole* and also a bawdy reference to the female sex organ.
20	*small* slim
26	*an old woman*. The F text has *a would-woman*. The commonest emendation is 'a wood woman' (meaning 'a mad woman'), but this is inappropriate in the context and it is difficult to see how such an error came about. Another suggestion is 'a wold woman' (meaning 'a country woman'). However, if Shakespeare had written 'a nould woman' the F reading would be understandable as a misprint for 'a nould' meaning 'an old'. The comic business is fairly clear:

Launce makes the shoe representing his mother give out a squeaking sound *up and down* like an asthmatic old woman. He admits that the imitation is not a perfect one, and by manipulating the shoe makes it more plausible.

27–8   *up and down* exactly. It has also been suggested that the reference is to the lacing of the shoe.

28–9   *Mark the moan she makes.* Launce presumably swishes the staff through the air as he says this.

30   *lay the dust* keep down the dust (by sprinkling it with tears)

32   *post* hasten

35, 36   *tied* (the dog which is) tied. The F spelling is *tide*.

44   *lose*. The two meanings suggested are 'lose' and 'loose, release'.

45–6   PANTHINO *Where should I lose my tongue?* LAUNCE *In thy tale.* This was a common bawdy gibe which Shakespeare also uses in *The Taming of the Shrew*, II.1.213–15.

49   *and the tied.* Launce may here 'loose' the dog. *Loose* is the spelling form of both 'lose' and 'loose' in the F text.

52   *call* summon

54   *call me.* In his usual way Launce mistakes Panthino's *call* to mean 'call names'.

II.4.1   *Servant.* See note to II.1.95.

7   *knocked* struck

(stage direction) *Exit.* This *Exit* does not occur in the F text, but it is clearly impracticable in terms of staging to have the clown on the stage during the subsequent exchange between the other characters, although some editors allow him to remain. See An Account of the Text, page 201.

12   *counterfeits* cheats

18   *quote* observe, note. The word was often written and

pronounced 'cote', which enables Valentine to pun
with 'coat' (*jerkin*) in line 19.

20   *jerkin ... doublet.* Both were articles of Elizabethan
clothing; the jerkin was a long jacket worn over a
doublet or in place of it, the doublet was a short and
loose coat-like garment.

21   *double.* The pun is with *doublet* (double it).

22   *How?* (an expression of surprise or annoyance)

27   *live in your air.* See note to II.1.163–4.

34   *giver* direction-giver (technically a person who
directed an archer's or gunner's aim)

36   *fire.* Valentine maintains the shooting allusions suggested by Silvia's *volley of words* in line 32.

38   *kindly* of natural affection or gratitude

43   *liveries* (uniforms worn by a gentleman's servants)

51   *happy messenger* bringer of good news

54   *worthy* worthy of

55   *without desert* undeservingly

61   *conversed* associated

63   *Omitting* neglecting, letting slip

68   *unmellowed* not tinged with grey hair

70   *Comes.* The singular verb form with a plural subject
is frequent in Shakespeare's grammar.

71   *feature* person, physical appearance

73   *Beshrew me* (a mild oath used for emphasis)

75   *meet* fitted

83   *cite* urge, summon. This F reading is sometimes taken
to be an abbreviation of 'incite' or 'excite' both of
which are incorrect.

84   *presently* now

88   *Belike* it is likely

       enfranchised set free

89   *pawn for fealty* pledge for fidelity

94   *Love hath not an eye at all.* See note to II.1.67.

96   *homely* plain

       wink shut the eye

102   *entertain* take into service

107   *discourse*. The accent is on the second syllable.

110   *want* lack

       meed reward

112   *die on him* challenge him to mortal combat, die fighting him

113   (stage direction) *Enter a Servant*. In the F text line 114 is given to Thurio. Such a reading requires that he exit some time earlier and re-enter here, which is how many editors solve the difficulty. Silvia's line 115 appears to be addressed to two separate people and so I have introduced the servant to issue the summons to Silvia from her father. The silence of Thurio in the preceding lines is certainly an unsatisfactory aspect of the scene but not altogether surprising in view of the fool he is.

121   *have them much commended* have sent their kind remembrances

127   *contemning* despising

128   *high imperious thoughts*. Cupid's imperiousness in dealing with lovers was sufficiently commonplace to make the F reading acceptable, although it has been suggested that the phrase is not appropriate and that the manuscript from which F was set may have had 'thonges'.

135   *as* that

136   *to* comparable to

142   *Was this the idol that you worship so?* This is ironical in view of Proteus's desire in IV.2.116–22 to worship Silvia's portrait.

149   *by her* of her

150   *principality*. This refers to the seventh order in the Christian hierarchy of divine beings below God. Dr Johnson with great ingenuity took the phrase to mean 'the first and principal of women'.

152   *Sweet*. This was a general term of affection applicable to men as well as women.

153   *Except* unless

except against take exception to, object to

155 *prefer* promote, advance in station. Valentine is quibbling on Proteus's *prefer* (meaning 'have a preference for') in line 154.

160 *to root* to receive the roots of

163 *can* can say

165 *alone* peerless, unique

170 *dream on thee* think about your feelings

173 *for* because

184 *inquire you forth* seek you out, ask after your whereabouts

185 *road.* See note to I.1.53.

187 *presently* immediately

190–93 *Even as one heat another heat expels . . . quite forgotten.* Arthur Brooke's poem *The Tragical History of Romeus and Juliet* (1562), which has been suggested as a possible source for part of the play, has: 'And as out of a plank a nail a nail doth drive, | So novel love out of the mind the ancient love doth rive.'

194 *Is it mine eye, or Valentine's praise.* The F reading *It is mine, or Valentine's praise* needs some emendation, the error having come about possibly through some cutting of the text, for the details of which, see An Account of the Text, pages 202–3. For the reasons for my preference of 'mine eye', see Introduction, pages 16–17. For other suggested emendations, see Collations 2. See also headnote to II.6.

205, 206 *advice* knowledge

207 *'Tis but her picture I have yet beheld.* If *picture* means 'portrait' here, then clearly there is something wrong with the text. Some editors explain away the difficulty by taking the word to mean 'outward appearance' as opposed to 'mind' (inner qualities). However, this is unacceptable in view of line 209. For a possible explanation of the origin of the difficulty, see An Account of the Text, page 202, and Introduction, pages 26–8.

208   *dazzlèd* (pronounced with three syllables)

210   *no reason but* no doubt that

212   *compass* obtain, win

II.5.1   *Milan*. The F text has *Padua* which is clearly erro-
neous. For details of the confused geography of
the play, see An Account of the Text, page 203.

3   *undone* ruined

5   *shot* tavern-reckoning, account

    hostess (hostess of a tavern)

8   *presently* at once

10   *part with* take leave of

11   *closed*. The quibble is on the two meanings: 'came to
terms' and 'embraced'.

17   *are they broken?* have they fallen out? is their affair
broken off?

18   *as whole as a fish* quite sound

19   *how stands the matter with them?* what is the state of
affairs between them?

20–21   *when it stands well with him, it stands well with her*.
Launce answers Speed's question literally: 'what is
agreeable to him is likewise agreeable to her', but he
also makes a bawdy joke by means of a quibble:
'when he has a sexual erection she is pleased by it.'

23   *block* blockhead

23–4   *My staff understands me*. With some bawdy gesture
Launce illustrates his quibble in lines 20–21.

26   *lean*. The quibble is on the two meanings: 'to put
one's weight on' and 'to incline in thought, affection,
or conduct'.

27   *understands*. The quibble is on the two meanings:
'supports' and 'comprehends'.

35   *by a parable* indirectly

36–7   *how sayest thou that my master is become* what have
you got to say about the fact that my master has become

40   *lubber* a large stupid man (with a pun on *lover*)

41   *whoreson* (a coarse pleasantry)

       thou mistakest me you misunderstand me

42–3 *I meant not thee, I meant thy master*. Launce thinks
       Speed is using *mistakest* with the meaning 'mistake
       (Speed) for (Valentine)'.

46   *If thou wilt, go with me to the alehouse*. The insertion
       of the comma after *wilt* makes good sense of the F
       line. There is no need, as some editors have done, to
       emend by following F2 and using *If thou wilt go with
       me to the alehouse, so*.

51   *the ale*. The reference is to a 'Church-ale' or a
       'Holy-ale' which were parish festivals (and thus
       Christian) at which ale was made and sold to raise
       church funds.

II.6   It has been suggested that Shakespeare in this scene
       was influenced by a passage in Sir Thomas Elyot's
       The Book of the Governor (1531) where the story of
       Titus and Gisippus is told. Titus falls in love with
       Gisippus's mistress, Sophronia: 'But Titus forthwith
       as he beheld so heavenly a personage adorned with
       beauty inexplicable, in whose visage was most
       amiable countenance mixed with maidenly shame-
       facedness . . . was thereat abashed, and had the heart
       through pierced with the fiery dart of blind Cupid.
       Of the which wound the anguish was so exceeding
       and vehement, that neither the study of philosophy,
       neither the remembrance of his dear friend Gisippus,
       who so much loved and trusted him, could anything
       withdraw him from that unkind appetite, but that of
       force he must love inordinately that lady, whom his
       said friend had determined to marry. Albeit with
       incredible pains he kept his thoughts secret' (page
       213).

1, 2   *forsworn*. Followed in this edition by semi-colons,

although F and some modern editors punctuate with
question marks. However, Proteus is rather pondering what he intends to do and the implications of his
actions than asking himself whether he should do so
or not.

7   *sweet-suggesting* sweetly tempting, seductive

12   *wit* sense

13   *learn* teach

17   *leave to love* stop loving

26   *Ethiope.* This was a common Elizabethan word for a
         black African, and was often used by Shakespeare as
         the antithesis of the English ideal of fair-skinned
         beauty. Compare *A Midsummer Night's Dream*,
         III.2.257; *Much Ado About Nothing*, V.4.38.

35   *competitor* associate, confederate

37   *pretended* intended

40   *cross* thwart

41   *blunt* stupid
         dull obtuse

43   *wit* ingenuity
         drift scheme

II.7   The parallel passage in *La Diana* is where Felismena
         (Julia) says she 'determined to adventure that which
         I think never any woman imagined: which was to
         apparel myself in the habit of a man, and to hie
         me to the court to see him in whose sight all my
         hope and content remained. Which determination I
         no sooner thought of than I put in practice, love
         blinding my eyes and mind with an inconsiderate
         regard of mine own estate and condition. To the
         execution of which attempt I wanted no industry.
         For, being furnished with the help of one of my
         approved friends and treasuress of my secrets, who
         bought me such apparel as I willed her and a good
         horse for my journey, I went not only out of my

country but out of my dear reputation; which I think I shall never recover again. And so trotted directly to the court, passing by way many accidents' (*Elizabethan Love Stories*, pages 136–7). Contrast the similar scene between Portia and Nerissa in *The Merchant of Venice*, III.4.

2   *conjure* beseech, adjure. The accent is on the first syllable.

3   *table* tablet for memoranda

4   *charactered* inscribed, written. The accent is on the second syllable.

5   *lesson* teach
     mean method

6   *with my honour* while preserving my honour

9   *true-devoted pilgrim*. This is another example of the religious love vocabulary of the play. Compare Valentine's words at I.1.52, II.4.143–51.

9–10 *weary | To measure* weary in traversing

16   *dearth* scarcity, famine

18   *inly* inward

22   *fire's* (two syllables)

24   *The more thou dammest it up, the more it burns*. Some editors have taken exception to the mixed metaphor here, although *dammest* could quite easily mean the 'banking' or 'piling up' of a fire with fuel.

28   *enamelled* variegated

29   *sedge* plant

32   *wild*. Some editors have found the word (in its meaning 'tempestuous') inappropriate because Julia parallels the *ocean* with her love, where like the *stream* she will *rest as . . . A blessèd soul doth in Elysium*. However, the word also meant simply 'open, wide, unenclosed'.
     ocean (pronounced with three syllables here)

38   *Elysium* (in Greek mythology, the abode of the blessed after death)

39   *habit* dress, clothing

40   *prevent* avoid (by taking preventative action)
41   *encounters* accostings
42   *weeds* garments
43   *beseem* be suitable for, be appropriate to
46   *odd-conceited* elaborately odd
47   *fantastic* fanciful, capricious
48   *greater time* older years
        show appear
51   *compass* circumference
        farthingale (hooped petticoat)
53   *must needs* will have to
        codpiece (a bagged covering over the male genitals at
        the front of close-fitting breeches)
54   *ill-favoured* ill-looking, unbecoming
55   *round hose* (breeches which covered both the loins
        and legs and puffed out at the hips)
        not worth a pin not at all valued
56   *to stick pins on* (one of the uses to which the codpiece
        was put)
58   *meet* suitable, appropriate
59   *how will the world repute me* what will people think of
        my action
60   *unstaid* immodest
61   *scandalized* disgraced, subject to scandal
64   *infamy* discredit
66   *No matter* it does not matter
67   *withal* with it
70   *of infinite of love.* There is no need for emendation
        here, as *infinite* as a noun meaning 'infinity' was
        common at the time.
74–81   *But truer stars did govern Proteus' birth . . . his truth.*
        Note how the dramatic effectiveness of this is
        heightened by its following immediately on Proteus's
        soliloquy in II.6.
74   *truer stars did govern Proteus' birth.* The allusion is to
        the belief that a man's character was determined by
        the astrological signs under which he was born.

79	*prove so* turn out to be so
81	*hard* bad
83	*presently* immediately
85	*longing* prompted by longing
86	*at thy dispose* in your charge, at your disposal
87	*reputation.* This is pronounced with five syllables.
90	*tarriance* delay

III.1.1	*give us leave* (a courteous form of dismissal)
2	(stage direction) *Exit Thurio.* This stage direction appears necessary although it does not appear in F. The entry and immediate exit of Thurio here appear purposeless, and have been adduced as evidence for the F text being a cut version of the play; see An Account of the Text, page 202.
4	*discover* disclose, reveal
8	*pricks me on* urges me
12	*am one made privy to* am one of the secret participants in
18	*drift* scheme, purpose
21	*timeless* untimely
25	*Haply* by chance
28	*jealous aim* suspicious guess
34	*suggested* tempted, led astray
35	*upper tower* the upper storey of a tower
36	*ever* always
38	*mean* method
40	*corded ladder* rope-ladder
42	*presently* immediately
45	*discovery* disclosure
	aimèd at guessed
46	*For. For* followed by a comma is the punctuation of the F text, indicating that the word means 'because' here. The large majority of modern editors omit the comma.

47	*publisher* one who exposes or brings to light
	pretence scheme, intention
49	*light* information
55	*of much import* of great significance. The accent in *import* is on the second syllable.
57	*happy being* agreeable life
59	*break with thee of* disclose to you
60	*touch me near* are of importance to me
66	*Beseeming* befitting
67	*fancy* love
68	*peevish* foolishly wayward
	froward refractory, rebellious, perverse
70	*regarding* taking due notice
73	*Upon advice* on reflection, on consideration
74	*where* whereas
77	*who* whoever
81	*of Verona.* The F text has *in Verona,* which is obviously incorrect. Many editors have attempted to solve the difficulty by substituting some form of 'Milan' that will not affect the metre (see Collations 2). I find this reading preferable as it gives the Duke a motive for approaching Valentine, another Veronese, on the subject.
82	*affect* am fond of
	nice fastidious
84	*to* as, for
85	*agone* ago
	forgot forgotten how
87	*bestow* conduct, deport
89	*respect not* takes no heed of
90–105	*Dumb jewels often in their silent kind . . . win a woman.* Note the change to rhymed couplets as the subject matter of the dialogue moves to the topic of Petrarchistic love-making. This is a more simple use of the device employed in *Romeo and Juliet* (I.5.93–106) where the lovers' initial exchange takes the form of a sonnet.

90   *kind* nature

91   *quick* lively or living (as opposed to the *Dumb* jewels of line 90)

93   *contents* pleases, delights

99   *For why* because

99–101   *the fools are mad if left alone . . . doth not mean 'Away!'* This appears to have been influenced by John Lyly's play *Sapho and Phao* (I.4.43–7): 'We are mad wenches, if men mark our words; for when I say, I would none cared for love more than I, what mean I but I would none loved but I? Where we cry "away", do we not presently say "go to"; and when men strive for kisses, we exclaim, "let us alone", as though we would fall to that ourselves.'

99   *fools* (a term of affection at the time)

101   *For* by

102–5   *Flatter and praise, commend, extol their graces . . . a woman.* John Lyly elaborates the idea in a similar way in *Sapho and Phao* (II.4.60–71): 'Flatter I mean lie. . . . Imagine with thyself all are to be won. . . . It is unpossible for the brittle metal of women to withstand the flattering attempts of men. . . . Be prodigal in praises. . . . There is none so foul, that thinketh not herself fair. In commending thou canst lose no labour; for of every one thou shalt be believed.'

103   *black* dark-complexioned (and thus, by contemporary English standards of beauty, not fair-skinned, not beautiful)

104, 105   *no man . . . woman.* A rhyme is almost certainly intended here.

109   *That* so that

110   *I would* I advise, I recommend

112   *That* so that

113   *lets* hinders, prevents

115   *shelving* overhanging

116   *apparent* obvious, evident, manifest

117   *quaintly* deftly, skilfully

119–20   *another Hero's tower, | So bold Leander would adven-*
          ture it. See note to I.1.22.

120   *So* provided
          adventure venture

121   *of blood* of good parentage. The phrase could also
          mean 'spirited', which is appropriate here.

130   *of any length* tolerably long

131   *turn* occasion

133   *such another* a similar

138   *engine* contrivance, instrument (the rope-ladder)
          proceeding scheme

140–49   *My thoughts do harbour with my Silvia nightly . . .*
          should be. The form of this poem suggests a regular
          Shakespearian sonnet without the final quatrain.

140–41   *My thoughts do harbour with my Silvia nightly, | And*
          slaves they are to me, that send them flying. Compare
          Sonnet 27: 'For then my thoughts, from far where I
          abide, | Intend a zealous pilgrimage to thee.'

140   *harbour* lodge

142   *lightly* easily

143   *senseless* insensible (of the honour)

144   *herald* bearing messages
          in thy pure bosom. The reference here is to the small
          pocket which Elizabethan women's gowns had
          located in the inside of the bodice between the
          breasts. It is frequently alluded to as a receptacle for
          letters, love-tokens, and sentimental mementoes.

145   *importune* command. The accent is on the second
          syllable.

146   *grace . . . grace* graciousness . . . favour. There may be
          in the first *grace* a quibble with 'one of the Graces'.

147   *want* lack

148   *I curse myself, for they are sent by me* in cursing them I
          am cursing myself who sent them (to the coveted
          resting-place)

153–5   *Why, Phaethon – for thou art Merops' son – . . . the*
          world? Phaethon was the son of Phoebus, the sun

god, by Clymene, the wife of Merops. He persuaded his father to let him drive the sun chariot, and, being unable to control the horses, allowed the chariot to come too near the earth. It has been suggested that there is a pun intended on *Merops* and 'ropes'.

156   *Wilt thou reach stars, because they shine on thee?* (a common proverb)

157   *overweening* presumptuous

158   *mates* (used scornfully here)

160   *Is privilege for* grants the privilege of

164   *expedition* haste, dispatch

170–87   *And why not death, rather than living torment? ... from life.* This is very similar in wording and sentiment to Romeo's complaint to Friar Laurence when he is banished for killing Tybalt in *Romeo and Juliet*, III.3.12–71: 'Ha, banishment? Be merciful, say "death". | For exile hath more terror in his look, | Much more than death.' (lines 12–14); 'There is no world without Verona walls ... | Hence banishèd is banished from the world ... | Heaven is here, | Where Juliet lives.' (lines 17, 19, 29–30).

175–7   *What joy is joy, if Silvia be not by? ... shadow of perfection.* This is exactly what Proteus elects to do in IV.2.116–22.

177   *shadow* illusion, image, idea

182   *essence* very life
         leave cease

183   *influence.* The allusion is to the *influence* exerted by a star on human beings, which was the basis of astrological belief.

185–7   *I fly not death, to fly his deadly doom ... from life.* Compare the similar quibbling in *Romeo and Juliet* (III.3.40–42, 44): 'This may flies do, when I from this must fly. | And sayest thou yet that exile is not death? | But Romeo may not, he is banishèd. ... | They are free men. But I am banishèd.'

185   *I fly not death, to fly his deadly doom.* The meaning

here is not altogether clear. Valentine may mean 'I do not escape death by running away from the Duke's sentence of death' or 'I do not escape death by flying away from death's deadly doom'.

to fly in flying

186   *attend on* wait for

187   At this point it has been suggested by some critics that an interval scene originally followed Valentine's soliloquy, because during these eighteen lines it is too much to believe that the Duke has issued a proclamation (lines 216–18), has interviewed Silvia (lines 221–32), and has imprisoned his daughter in the tower (lines 233–6).

189   *So-ho*. This was the hunter's cry when a hare was started.

191–2 *there's not a hair on's head but 'tis a Valentine* every hair on his head declares him for what he is: namely, a true lover

191   *a hair*. Launce is punning on 'hare', which, with his cry in line 189, he pretended to be hunting.

192   *a Valentine*. Launce quibbles on Valentine's name and its meaning, 'a token of true love'. Compare lines 210–14.

208   *they. News* is being thought of as plural.

211   *No Valentine*. The quibble is on the two meanings: 'no longer myself' and 'no true love'.

216   *proclamation*. The proclamation of Valentine's banishment, Silvia's interview with her father, and her imprisonment in the tower have all taken place in the time covered by Valentine's soliloquy at lines 170–87. This has persuaded some editors that the text has been cut at this point; see An Account of the Text, page 203. However, it should be noticed that there are similar time anomalies in Shakespeare's other plays.

vanished (a malapropism for 'banished')

220   *surfeit* sicken from over-abundance

222   *doom* sentence

233   *chafed* irritated, enraged

234   *repeal* recall

240   *anthem* song of grief, requiem

247   *manage* handle, wield

250   *Even in the milk-white bosom.* See note to line 144.

251   *expostulate* discuss, expatiate

255   *though not for thyself* even though not for your own
           sake

256   *Regard* take notice of

262–3   *but that's all one if he be but one knave.* Behind
           Launce's remark seems to lie the proverb 'Two
           knaves need no broker'. 'Two knaves' was a common
           term in reference to excessive knavery at the time
           (compare *Othello*, I.3.388: 'double knavery'). Some
           editors have thought the reference may be to Proteus
           – a knave to both his mistress and his friend.

263–4   *He lives not now that knows me to be in love.* This may
           be an allusion to Valentine's disclosure of his affairs to
           Proteus.

264   *horse* horses

267–8   *yet 'tis not a maid, for she hath had gossips. Gossips*
           were originally a child's baptismal sponsors; how-
           ever, the word came to mean in common parlance
           'women friends invited to attend a birth'. Launce
           implies that his inamorata is not a virgin (*maid*) as
           she has had an illegitimate child.

268   *maid* servant (the quibble being with *maid* (meaning
           'virgin') in line 267)

269–70   *more qualities than a water-spaniel.* The spaniel was
           proverbial for its fawning. The many uses of the
           water-spaniel are listed in Dr Caius's *Treatise on*
           English Dogs (1576), among which are the capacity to
           find hidden duck by the smell, to locate and recover
           spent bolts and arrows which have dropped into the
           water, and to bring back to the hunter both the ducks
           he has shot and the ducks killed by other means.

270   *bare*. Launce implies the two meanings: 'mere' and 'naked' (as opposed to the hair-covered spaniel).

271   *cate-log* catalogue. Some editors modernize the spelling, pointing out correctly that 'catlog' was a recognized spelling at the time. However, there are the possibilities that (1) the spelling was intended to indicate Launce's pronunciation, and (2) a quibble is intended with 'cates' (meaning 'dainties').
       condition qualities

271-4 *Imprimis ... carry. ... Item ... milk*. The form adopted here is that of the usual Elizabethan inventory of goods.

272-3 *a horse cannot fetch*. The verb means 'go and bring' which a horse cannot be ordered to do.

274   *jade*. Launce quibbles on the two meanings: 'a woman of low morals' and 'a mare in bad physical condition'.

278   *master's ship*. The F text has *Mastership*, but the pun is obviously intended.
       at sea. The quibble is on the two meanings: 'afloat' and 'awry'.

279   *old vice still*. It has been suggested that there is an allusion here to the 'Vice' (a combination of clown and villain) of the old Morality plays which were performed in England up to the 1570s.

282   *black* bad

284   *them*. See note to line 208.

285   *jolt-head* blockhead, numbskull

289   *loiterer* idler

292   *Saint Nicholas be thy speed!* may Saint Nicholas help you! (with a pun on Speed's name). Saint Nicholas was the legendary patron saint of scholars.

293-4 SPEED *Imprimis: She can milk*. LAUNCE *Ay, that she can*. Launce is quibbling on the second meaning of *milk*: 'to entice a lover by wiles'. It is noticeable that Speed quotes differently from Launce so far as the beginning of the catalogue is concerned.

294   *can* (possibly a pun on 'milk-can')

301   *stock* dowry

302   *knit him a stock* knit him a stocking or netherstock. Launce is also playing on *knit* meaning 'conceive' and *stock* which could mean both 'a stupid person' and 'a line of descendants'.

305   *washed and scoured*. The quibble is on the meanings 'knocked down' and 'beaten'.

307–8   *she can spin for her living*. The verb may carry a sexual connotation as it does in *Twelfth Night*, I.3.99.

307   *set the world on wheels* live at ease, let things slide, be independent

309   *nameless* inexpressible (but carrying overtones also of 'too small to be worth detailed description')

310   *bastard virtues* virtuous qualities of little value, inferior or base virtues

313–14   SPEED *Here follow her vices.* LAUNCE *Close at the heels of her virtues.* It is possible that this is an allusion to the alternating vice and virtue scenes in the old Morality plays.

313   *Here follow her vices.* Some editors take this to be a quotation from Launce's catalogue.

315   *to be kissed fasting*. The F text reads *to be fasting*. It has been suggested that the blank was left deliberately for the clown to supply an *ad lib.* indecency; but Launce's reply seems to require this universally accepted emendation from Rowe's edition of 1709.
        in respect of owing to, on account of

319   *a sweet mouth* a wanton or lecherous nature. It is not altogether clear whether Launce takes this literally to mean 'a kissable mouth' which compensates for her bad breath.

322–3   *sleep not in her talk* is not slow or stupid in her speech. There is also a quibble intended on *sleep* and 'slip' similar to that on *sheep* and 'ship' at I.1.73.

329   *it was Eve's legacy*. Launce may merely mean that

pride was the original deadly sin, or he may be taking
proud to mean 'hot-blooded, lascivious'.

332   *because I love crusts* (and will not have to share them
with her)

333   *curst* shrewish

335   *praise* appraise, test (by sipping)

336   *If her liquor be good, she shall.* Launce takes *praise* to
mean 'laud'.

338   *liberal* bold, wanton, loose in her talk

341   *another thing* (a sexual allusion)

343-4   *She hath more hair than wit, and more faults than
hairs.* It has been suggested that this is a parody of a
passage in John Lyly's *Euphues, The Anatomy of Wit*
(1578): 'This young gallant of more wit than wealth,
and yet of more wealth than wisdom' (page 1).

343   *more hair than wit* (a proverbial expression)

346   *Rehearse* repeat

349-50   *the cover of the salt hides the salt* the lid of the salt-
cellar conceals the salt. The quibble is on *salt* meaning 'wit'.

356   *gracious* acceptable

360   *stays* waits

366   *Thou must run to him.* Launce takes Speed's word *go*
to mean 'walk', which was a common Elizabethan
meaning.

        stayed tarried

367   *going* walking

        serve the turn be appropriate

370   *swinged* thrashed, beaten

372   *correction* punishment

III.2.3-5   *Since his exile she hath despised me most . . . obtaining
her.* It might be assumed from this that there has been
a lapse of some time between III.1 and III.2; but it
is clear from lines 11-13 that the time-lapse is but a

few hours. The accent is on the second syllable in *exile*.

5   *That* so that
       desperate without hope

6   *impress*. The accent is on the second syllable.

7   *Trenchèd* cut
       hour's (pronounced with two syllables here)

8   *his* its
       form shape

14   *grievously* sorrowfully. Some copies of F have *heavily*, which is on the uncorrected version of the page.

17   *conceit* conception, opinion

19   *better* more ready, more willing

28   *persevers* perseveres. The accent is on the second syllable.

35   *deliver* report

36   *circumstance* much incidental detail, circumlocution

41   *very friend* true or special friend

44   *is indifferent* counts neither way, is neither good nor bad

45   *your friend* (the Duke)

49   *weed* weed out, root out. Chiefly because of Thurio's word *unwind* in line 51, many editors have felt disposed to emend this word. The suggestions made include 'wind', 'wend', and 'woo'.

52   *ravel* become entangled

53   *bottom it* wind it. A skein or ball of wool was wound on a core or 'bottom' of some harder material.

56   *in this kind* in an affair of this kind

58   *You are already Love's firm votary.* Note the irony.

60   *Upon this warrant* in accordance with this command

62   *lumpish* low-spirited, in the dumps

64   *temper* mould, dispose

67   *sharp* keen

68   *lime* bird-lime. It is noticeable that Proteus's metaphor is one of trapping.
       tangle ensnare

70   *serviceable vows* devoted vows or vows of service

77   *discover such integrity* disclose such true devotion. Some editors have hazarded that a line has been lost following this. However, *such* may refer to the devotion which would result if the advice in the foregoing lines was followed, or possibly to the tears used to moisten the ink.

78–81   *For Orpheus' lute was strung with poets' sinews . . . on sands.* The allusion is to the mythical Greek musician to whom were attributed the powers described.

78   *sinews* nerves

81   *unsounded* unfathomable

82   *elegies* love poems

83   *Visit* go with some accompaniment

84   *consort* company of musicians (usually referring to those who performed part-songs). The accent is on the first syllable.

85   *dump* sad tune

86   *grievance* grieving, grief, or sorrowful affections

87   *inherit* secure, gain possession of

88   *This discipline shows thou hast been in love.* Note the irony in the use of the past tense of the verb.
        discipline instruction, lesson

90   *direction-giver.* See note to II.4.34.

91   *presently* immediately

92   *sort* sort out, select

94   *To give the onset to* to make a beginning in following

98   *Even now about it!* do it immediately! (not after supper)
        pardon you excuse your attendance on me

IV.1   This scene obviously takes place in a forest on the outskirts of Milan and, presumably, in the direction of Verona.

1   *passenger* traveller

4	*sit* (in weak antithesis to *stand* in line 3)
	rifle plunder, search and rob
5	*undone* come to grief
10	*by my beard* (a common oath of the time)
	proper handsome, comely
12	*crossed with* thwarted by
20	*sixteen months*. This is an example of the confused time-scheme of the play, as it would entail a time-lapse of some fifteen months between I.1 and I.3.
21	*crooked* malignant
25	*rehearse* repeat
28	*Without false vantage* in an equal match, fairly
31	*held me glad of such a doom* considered myself lucky to be given such a sentence (instead of the death penalty)
32	*Have you the tongues?* can you speak foreign languages?
33	*travel*. The F text has *trauaile* which was used interchangeably with 'travel' for both meanings. Therefore, although, strictly speaking, there is some doubt whether Valentine is attributing his linguistic skill to 'travel' or 'travail' (that is, work or study) in his youth, the latter seems unlikely in the context.
	happy facile, proficient
35	*fat friar* (Friar Tuck of the Robin Hood legend)
36	*were* would be
41–2	*anything to take to* any means of subsistence
46	*awful* law-abiding, commanding respect. There is some plausibility in the suggestion that the compositor simply misread 'lawful', as there is no apparent reason for this particular word. However, the writing is such wretched stuff that it is useless to attempt to justify any word on literary grounds.
48	*practising* plotting, scheming
49	*An heir, and near allied unto the Duke*. The F reading *And heire, and Neece, alide vnto the Duke* is usually emended in this way, on the grounds that the com-

positor probably misread 'neece' for 'neere' which was a common error and one which may have occurred in reverse in *King John*, II.1.424.

heir. This could be used of both sexes.

51   *mood* fit of anger

58   *quality* profession, vocation

60   *the rest* any other reason

62   *To make a virtue of necessity* (a common proverb)

64   *consort* band, fellowship. The accent is on the second syllable.

69   *brag* report

72   *silly* simple (thus 'helpless' or 'harmless')

     poor passengers travellers without money

74   *crews* groups of confederates. It has been suggested that this is a misprint for 'caves' on the grounds that this would be more appropriate in view of line 75 and that a reference is made to a cave at V.3.12.

76   *dispose* disposal

IV.2   This scene would appear at first sight to follow on directly from III.2 in which Thurio announces his intention of serenading Silvia. However, it is clear from Proteus's opening speech that some days have elapsed in which he has made use of the Duke's permission to visit his daughter.

3   *colour* pretence

4   *prefer* urge, recommend

5   *holy* good, virtuous. See the echo of this in the song at line 40.

8   *twits* blames

9   *commend* deliver, offer

12-15   *And notwithstanding all her sudden quips . . . her still.* In *La Diana* it is noted of Felix (Proteus): 'the more he perceived that his lady forgot him, the more was his mind troubled with greater cares and grief which made him lead the most sorrowful life' (*Elizabethan Love Stories*, page 151).

12   *sudden quips* sharp taunts or sarcastic utterances

14   *spaniel-like* fawningly

18   *crept.* Note the appropriateness of this word, which implies slyness, in connexion with Proteus's character and behaviour.

19–20   *love | Will creep in service where it cannot go* (a common proverb)

20   *go* walk (as opposed to *creep*)

25–81   *Let's tune, and to it lustily awhile ... Farewell.* This whole musical incident is quite closely paralleled in *La Diana*: 'The great joy that I felt in hearing him cannot be imagined; for methought I heard him now as in that happy and past time of our loves. But after the deceit of this imagination was discovered, seeing with mine eyes and hearing with mine ears that this music was bestowed upon another and not on me, God knows what a bitter death it was unto my soul! And with a grievous sigh that carried almost my life away with it, I asked mine host if he knew what the lady was for whose sake the music was made. He answered me that he could not imagine on whom it was bestowed, because in that street dwelled many noble and fair ladies' (*Elizabethan Love Stories*, pages 138–9).

25   (stage direction) *Host of the Inn.* This character also figures largely in *La Diana*. The disguised Felismena (Julia) relates: 'Twenty days I was in going thither, at the end of which, being come to the desired place, I took up mine inn in a street least frequented with concourse of people' (*Elizabethan Love Stories*, page 137).

26   *allycholly.* This mistake for 'melancholy' was perhaps a common one among the lower classes, as Mistress Quickly makes the same one in *The Merry Wives of Windsor*, I.4.138.

34–68   (stage direction) *The Musicians play* . . . Compare
La Diana: '. . . they began to wind three cornets
and a sackbut with such skill and sweetness that
it seemed celestial music. And then began a voice
to sing, the sweetest, in my opinion, that ever I
heard. And though I was in suspense by hearing
Fabius speak, whereby a thousand doubts and
imaginations, repugnant to my rest, occurred in my
mind, yet I neglected not to hear what was sung,
because their operations were not of such force that
they were able to hinder the desire nor distemper the
delight that I conceived by hearing it' (*Elizabethan
Love Stories*, page 137).

37   *Song.* The whole serenade comprises (1) an instrumental introduction, (2) the song itself, (3) an instrumental postlude. Proteus presumably performs the
solo part. The song is justly one of the most popular
Shakespeare wrote. There is no extant contemporary
setting. It has been set to music by over fifty different
composers, including Thomas Arne, Edward Ger-
man, Roger Quilter, Eric Coates, and Edmund
Rubbra. The best, and best known, setting, of course,
is Schubert's.

39   *swains* young men

44   *For beauty lives with kindness* beauty flourishes in the
doing of generous actions

45   *repair* hasten

47   *inhabits* dwells

53–68   *How now? . . . but one thing.* The quibbling here is on
the correspondence, used by Shakespeare throughout
his career, between musical harmony (seen as the
earthly reflection of the harmony of the spheres) and
spiritual harmony in either the individual or the state
or the natural world. For a discussion of the dramatic
importance of this passage, see Introduction, pages
34–7.

54   *likes* pleases

55   *the musician likes me not.* Julia, meaning 'the musician does not love me', quibbles on the Host's use of the word *likes* in line 54.

57   *plays false.* The two meanings are: 'is unfaithful' and 'plays a wrong musical note'.

61   *a quick ear.* The Host still thinks that, because Julia has detected a wrong note in the serenade, she is musically discriminating.

62   *I would I were deaf.* Julia quibbles on the Host's word *quick* taking it to mean an 'alive' as opposed to a 'dead' or 'deaf' ear.

    slow heavy, dull. The meaning 'slow-beating' is opposed to *quick*.

65   *Not a whit* not at all

    jars grates

66   *change.* This was a technical term used to describe a variation or modulation in musical compositions.

67   *change* change of affections

    spite injury

69   *I would always have one play but one thing.* Julia means that she would have only Proteus as her lover. There is a bawdy overtone in the phrase as Shakespeare often used the word 'play' as a metaphor for a man's making love to a woman.

70–73   *But, host, doth this Sir Proteus, that we talk on . . . all nick.* Compare *La Diana*: 'To inquire of him of mine host I durst not, lest my coming might, perhaps, have been discovered' (*Elizabethan Love Stories*, page 137). Felismena (Julia) is informed of Felix's (Proteus's) passion by his page.

70   *talk on* talk of

73   *out of all nick* beyond all reckoning. The allusion is to the practice of keeping accounts or tallies by making 'nicks' or notches on a stick. It is thus an appropriate phrase to be found in an innkeeper's mouth, or, considering Launce's lines at II.5.3–6, equally typical of him.

75-7   *Gone to seek his dog, which tomorrow, by his master's*
        command, he must carry for a present to his lady.
        Launce does in fact present his dog to his master's
        lady (see IV.4.1–37), but it is not, as the Host says,
        by his master's command (see IV.4.43–57).

78   *parts* departs

80   *drift* scheme, intention

81   *Saint Gregory's Well.* There is, in fact, a well of this
        name near Milan.
        (stage direction) *at an upstairs window.* There is no
        general agreement among theatre historians as to the
        exact nature of the upper acting area of the Eliza-
        bethan stages. It would appear here that an open
        window rather than a balcony is all that is required.

89   *will* wish, desire
        compass yours gain your good will. Proteus's quibble
        is on the meaning 'perform your least wish'.

90-101 *You have your wish; my will is even this . . . talking*
        to thee. In *La Diana* Celia (Silvia) sends Felix
        (Proteus) a letter: '"For well thou mightest have
        denied, or not declared, thy past love, without
        giving me occasion to condemn thee by thine own
        confession. Thou sayest I was the cause that made
        thee forget thy former love. Comfort thyself; for
        there shall not want another to make thee forget thy
        second"' (*Elizabethan Love Stories*, page 145).

91   *presently* immediately

92   *subtle* crafty

93   *conceitless* witless, lacking understanding

94   *To be* as to be

97   *pale queen of night* the moon. The reference is to
        Diana, who was also the goddess of chastity, and thus
        an appropriate figure for Silvia to swear by in her
        present situation.

103   *'Twere false, if I should speak it.* It would be false even
        if Julia should say so who has the right to claim it in
        two possible senses: (1) that Julia is 'dead' now that

she is Sebastian; (2) that Julia might claim to have
been 'killed' by Proteus's unfaithfulness.

108   *importunacy*. The accent is on the third syllable.

114   *sepulchre*. The accent is on the second syllable.

115   *He heard not that* he will deliberately ignore that

116   *obdurate*. The accent is on the second syllable.

118   *The picture that is hanging in your chamber*. There
appears to be some connexion between this reference
and Proteus's words at II.4.207, to which see the
note. See also Introduction, pages 24–8.

120–22   *For since the substance of your perfect self . . . true love.*
Contrast this with Valentine's diametrically opposite
view on the same topic at III.1.174–7. See also
Introduction, pages 23–5.

120   *perfect* complete

121   *else* elsewhere, to another person
       shadow lifeless person

122   *shadow* image, portrait

124   *shadow*. The quibble is on the two meanings: 'a lifeless person' and 'a version of my true self' (as she is
in disguise).

125   *your idol*. Contrast Proteus's denial of Silvia's capacity
to inspire worship when it is claimed for her by
Valentine at II.4.142–45.

126   *since your falsehood shall become you well* since it shall
be most appropriate to your falsehood

127   *To worship shadows and adore false shapes*. The
allusion is to Proteus's name as well as to his nature.
See headnote to I.1.

132   *By my halidom*. The word *halidom* was used to
describe anything regarded as sacred.

133–6   *Pray you, where lies . . . most heaviest*. Compare
La Diana: 'About dawning of the day the music
ended; and I did what I could to espy out my Don
Felix. But the darkness of the night was mine
enemy therein. And seeing now that they were gone,
I went to bed again, where I bewailed my great

mishap, knowing that he whom most of all I loved
had so unworthily forgotten me; whereof his music
was too manifest a witness' (*Elizabethan Love
Stories*, page 140).

133   *lies* lodges
134   *house* inn
136   *watched* remained awake through
       most heaviest most depressing. The double superlative
       is common in Shakespeare's grammar.

IV.3   Some editors make this scene merely a continuation
        of IV.2. However, the scene is the day following and
        the stage is obviously intended to be cleared before
        the entrance of Eglamour.

8   *impose* command imposed
9   *thus early*. Therefore, not much later than the time
       when Julia and the Host left Silvia's window, when
       it was *almost day* (IV.2.134).
13   *Valiant, wise, remorseful, well-accomplished*. The
       metre is defective and there have been various sug-
       gestions made for correcting it (see Collations 2).
       remorseful pitiful, compassionate
14   *dear* affectionate
16   *enforce me marry* force me to marry
17   *Vain* empty, stupid
       abhors. The F text's *abhor'd* would appear to be a
       compositor's error, although it has been defended as
       a reference by Silvia to the time before she loved
       Valentine.
22   *I would to* I wish to go to
24   *for* because
26   *repose* rely
27   *Urge not* do not bring forward as an excuse (for not
       doing what I wish)
30-31 *a most unholy match, | Which heaven and fortune still
       rewards with plagues*. Note the religious vocabulary

used here in connexion with love, as it is elsewhere in the play.

31   *rewards*. The singular verb form with two singular subjects is common in Shakespeare's grammar.

37   *grievances*. This word is usually glossed here as 'distresses, injuries' which in view of the following line appears to me to be impossible. Dr Johnson's suggestion 'sorrowful affections' which are *virtuously . . . placed* with Valentine is far more likely. The word is used in this sense also at III.2.86.

40   *Recking* caring
      betideth befalls

41   *befortune* befall, betide

44   *confession* (pronounced with four syllables here)

IV.4   It is obvious from line 83 that, as in IV.3, the scene is before Silvia's tower. However, Eglamour departs at dawn, whereas Launce enters after dinner (i.e. after noon). From this it has been suggested that a scene has been omitted between IV.3 and IV.4.

1–37   *When a man's servant . . . a trick?* For the relevance of this speech to the main plot, see Introduction, pages 33–4.

2   *of* from

4   *to it* to drowning, to death

4–6   *I have taught him, even as one would say precisely, 'Thus I would teach a dog.'* I follow F punctuation; for the suggested alternative reading see Collations 2.

8   *steps me*. The expletive *me* indicates that an interest in the proceedings was felt by the person indicated. See also the same usage at lines 16 and 23.

9   *trencher* wooden plate
      capon's chicken's

10   *keep himself* restrain himself, exercise self-control

12   *a dog at* adept at

13–14   *to take a fault upon me* to take the blame for the fault
        myself

18   *bless the mark*. This phrase was used parenthetically
        as an apology when something unacceptable was
        being said. Originally it was a formula for averting
        evil omens.

        a pissing while. This was a colloquial term meaning
        'a very short time'. However, Launce also means it
        literally: 'the duration of time necessary for Crab to
        urinate'.

23   *the fellow that whips the dogs* (the kennel man)

26   *wot* know

29   *stocks* (a common punishment for acts of theft)

        puddings (a savoury dish made of stuffed animal
        intestines)

31   *pillory*. In the pillory the prisoner was fastened by the
        head and hands, as opposed to the stocks in which he
        was fastened by the legs.

34   *Madam Silvia*. It is possible that this should be
        'Madam Julia', considering that Launce, in the
        incident as he describes it, would have had little
        opportunity for 'taking leave' of Silvia. Also Launce
        is asking Crab to remember, which suggests that he is
        referring to a previous incident.

39   *presently* straight away

41   *whoreson* (a coarse pleasantry)

45   *jewel*. F has this word capitalized which may suggest
        that the dog's name is indicated. This is a possibility,
        although the capitalization practice of F does not
        merit such confidence.

47   *currish* ignoble, mean-spirited. The pun is with *cur*
        in line 46.

52   *squirrel*. This is an indication of the size of the dog,
        but the word has also been taken to be the name of the
        dog.

53   *hangman boys*. The F text has *Hangman's boyes*; but

the meaning is almost certainly 'boys fit for the hangman, roughnecks'.

54–5   *a dog as big as ten of yours.* Despite this line, in theatrical productions the dogs range from a small wretched animal to something resembling the Hound of the Baskervilles.

59   *still an end* continuously, perpetually

        turns me to shame brings shame upon me

60–86   *Sebastian, I have entertainèd thee . . . and solitary.* In *La Diana* Felismena (Julia) tells how she was employed by Felix (Proteus): '. . . Don Felix, as soon as he was come forth . . . commanded me the same night to come to him at his lodging. Thither I went, and he entertained me for his page, making the most of me in the world; where, being but a few days with him, I saw the messages, letters, and gifts that were brought and carried on both sides – grievous wounds, alas! and corsives to my dying heart. . . . But after one month was past, Don Felix began to like so well of me that he disclosed his whole love unto me, from the beginning unto the present estate and forwardness that it was then in, committing the charge thereof to my secrecy and help, telling me that he was favoured of her at the beginning, and that afterwards she waxed weary of her loving and accustomed entertainment, the cause whereof was a secret report (whosoever it was that buzzed it into her ears) of the love that he did bear to a lady in his own country. . . . "And there is no doubt," said Don Felix unto me, "but that indeed, I did once commence that love that she lays to my charge. But God knows if now there be anything in the world that I love and esteem more dear and precious than her." When I heard him say so, you may imagine . . . what a mortal dagger pierced my wounded heart. But with dissembling the matter the best I could, I answered him thus: "It were better, sir, methinks, that the gentlewoman should complain with cause, and that it were so indeed. For if the other lady, whom you served before, did not deserve to be forgotten of you, you do her (under correction, my lord) the greatest wrong in the world." "The love," said Don Felix again, "which I bear to my Celia will not let me understand it so. But I have done her, methinks, the greatest injury, having placed my love first in another, and not in her." "Of these wrongs," said I to myself, "I know who bears the worst away"' (*Elizabethan Love Stories*, pages 144–5).

60–69   *Sebastian, I have entertainèd thee . . . Silvia.* Compare Orsino's lines to Viola in *Twelfth Night* (I.4.24–36): 'O, then unfold the passion of my love. | Surprise her with discourse of my dear faith. | It shall become thee well to act my woes; | She will attend it better in thy youth | Than in a nuncio's of more grave aspect. . . . | For they shall yet belie thy happy years | That say thou art a man. Diana's lip | Is not more smooth and rubious. . . . | I know thy constellation is right apt | For this affair.' Orsino also sends Olivia a jewel by Viola.

60   *entertainèd* taken into service

64–6   *But chiefly for thy face and thy behaviour . . . truth.* It is ironical that Proteus should (a) so readily recognize these qualities in the face of his mistress, and (b) prize them so highly in view of his own behaviour.

65   *augury* prophetic skill

68   *presently* immediately

70   *well delivered* well (who) delivered

71   *to leave* to part with

72   *belike* in all likelihood

73–81   *Alas! . . . cry 'Alas!'.* Compare *La Diana*: '"If thy grief doth suffer any counsel," said I, "that thy thoughts be divided into this second passion, since there is so much due to the first." Don Felix answered me again, sighing, and knocking me gently

188

on the shoulder, saying: "How wise art thou,
Valerius, and what good counsel dost thou give me –
if I could follow it!" . . . "I think, sir, it is needless
to amend this letter, or to make the gentlewoman
amends to whom it is sent, but her whom you do
injury so much with it"' (*Elizabethan Love Stories*,
pages 146–7).

82   *therewithal* with it

83   *That's her chamber.* There has been a great deal of
discussion about the location of this scene, many
editors pointing out that there is an imaginary change
of place from outside to inside the tower after
Proteus's exit, which is necessary because Silvia is
a prisoner in the tower. Other editors have seen the
difficulty as resulting from abridgement of the text.
See An Account of the Text, pages 202–3.

90   *poor fool* (referring to herself)

96–9   *And now am I, unhappy messenger . . . dispraised.*
Compare Viola's speech in *Twelfth Night* (I.4.40–42):
'I'll do my best | To woo your lady. (*Aside*) Yet, a
barful strife! | Whoe'er I woo, myself would be his
wife.'

96–7   *And now am I, unhappy messenger, | To plead for that
which I would not obtain.* Compare Felismena's
similar lament in *La Diana*: '"O thrice unfortunate
Felismena, that with thine own weapons art con-
strained to wound thy ever-dying heart, and to heap
up favours for him who made so small account of
thine"' (*Elizabethan Love Stories*, pages 150–51).

98, 99   *would have* desire to have

100–104   *I am my master's true confirmèd love . . . him speed.*
Compare Viola's words in *Twelfth Night* (II.2.33–8):
'My master loves her dearly; | And I, poor monster,
fond as much on him . . . | My state is desperate for
my master's love. | As I am a woman – now, alas the
day . . . !'

104   *speed* succeed, prosper

105	*mean* agent, means
106	*where to speak* where I may speak
115–17	*Tell him from me . . . this shadow*. Silvia's attitude on the value of the image as opposed to the reality of the loved one is similar to Valentine's at III.1.174–84.
117	*shadow* image, portrait. Silvia probably also implies the meaning 'mere nothing'.
119	*unadvised* inadvertently
120	(stage direction) *Julia takes back the letter she offers and gives Silvia another one*. There seems little point in Julia first offering by mistake what is obviously one of Proteus's letters to herself and then handing Silvia the right one, unless in a fuller version of the play the idea was more completely developed.
127	*new-found* recently invented
137	*tender* have a tender regard for
139–69	*Dost thou know her? . . . very sorrow*. Compare *La Diana*: '"Dost thou then know Felismena," said Celia, "the lady whom thy master did once love and serve in his own country?" "I know her," said I, "although not so well as it was needful for me to have prevented so many mishaps" – and this I spake softly to myself – "for my father's house was near to hers." . . . Celia began in good earnest to ask me what manner of woman Felismena was; whom I answered that, touching her beauty, some thought her to be very fair; but I was never of that opinion, because she hath many days since wanted the chiefest thing that is requisite for it. "What is that?" said Celia. "Content of mind," said I, "because perfect beauty can never be where the same is not adjoined to it"' (*Elizabethan Love Stories*, page 149).
140–69	*Almost as well as I do know myself . . . very sorrow*. Julia's description of herself and Silvia's unawareness of the device is similar to that in which Viola describes her own love for Orsino under the guise of talking about her sister in *Twelfth Night* (II.4.106–8): 'My

father had a daughter loved a man – | As it might be perhaps, were I a woman, | I should your lordship.'

142 *several* different

143 *Belike* in all likelihood

150 *sun-expelling mask.* As the standard of feminine beauty in Elizabethan England was fair, the more fashionable and courtly women of the time protected their complexions against sunburn by means of masks or, more commonly, stiffened velvet headpieces called *bongraces.*

152 *lily-tincture* white colour

153 *That* so that
black dark-skinned (from sunburn)

155–69 *About my stature; for, at Pentecost . . . very sorrow.* For comment on these lines, see Introduction, pages 25–6.

155–6 *at Pentecost, | When all our pageants of delight were played.* Whitsuntide had long been associated with public celebrations in England. The religious Mystery Cycle plays had been performed at this time of the year in some parts of the country, as were May games, and (according to *The Winter's Tale*, IV.4.134) 'Whitsun pastorals'.

156 *pageants of delight* pleasant performances

157 *the woman's part.* All female roles were played by boys on the Elizabethan stage.

158 *trimmed* dressed

162 *agood* in earnest

164–5 *'twas Ariadne passioning | For Theseus' perjury and unjust flight.* Ariadne was the daughter of Minos, king of Crete. She fell in love with Theseus, prince of Sparta, and, after helping him slay the Minotaur, fled with him, only to be abandoned by him on the Isle of Naxos.

164 *passioning* sorrowing, passionately grieving

166 *lively* (adverbial)

170 *beholding* indebted

178 *cold* ineffectual, coldly received

182 *tire*. This was a term which was applied to women's head-dress generally, although Julia appears to be referring to the type of head-wear that set off the face, such as the French Hood or the reticulated caul or coif.

186 *auburn* whitish, flaxen
  perfect yellow. This was the natural colour of Queen Elizabeth I's hair and, consequently, a fashionable colour.

188 *a coloured periwig*. False hair was extensively used by Elizabethan women.

189 *grey*. The word was used to describe blue eyes.

190 *as high*. A high forehead was much admired as an aspect of female beauty.

192 *But I can* that I cannot
  respective worthy of respect, likely to inspire respect

193 *fond* foolishly doting

194 *shadow*. Julia can be considered such because of her disguise and because her treatment by Proteus has made her a 'lifeless version' of her former self.
  take ... up. The quibble is on the two meanings: 'pick up' and 'oppose, accept the challenge'.
  this shadow (the portrait of Silvia). See notes to IV.2.121, 122, 124.

195 *senseless* insensible

197 *sense* rational meaning

198 *statue*. Julia is setting herself as a substantial image against the *shadow* – the two-dimensional image of the painting.

199 *use* treat

V.1.6 *expedition* haste. This is pronounced with five syllables.

9 *postern* (small side door)

12   *recover* reach
        sure safe, secure

V.2.1–29   *Sir Proteus, what says Silvia to my suit? . . . by lease.*
           The same device for poking fun at a fool is used in
           Cymbeline, I.2, II.1.

3   *takes exceptions at* makes objections to, finds fault
        with
5   *too little.* Proteus's allusion is perhaps to Thurio's
        excessively thin legs.
6   *boot* riding-boot
7   JULIA. The F text assigns this line to Proteus, and
        lines 13–14 to Thurio. However, in view of the design
        of the scene, they are almost certainly comments by
        Julia on the conversation between the two men.
        spurred. The quibble is with *boot* (meaning 'riding-
        boot') in line 6.
9   *a fair one* pale or fresh-complexioned. The suggestion
        is thus one of effeminacy.
10   *black* swarthy
12   *Black men* dark-complexioned men
13   *pearls.* Julia quibbles on the proverb by taking the
        word *pearls* in its medical sense: 'cataracts'.
14   *wink* shut my eyes
16   *Ill, when you talk of war.* This also carries the sug-
        gestion of effeminacy.
20   *makes no doubt of that* does not question it (since
        Silvia, like Julia, has perceived its true quality)
23   *derived* descended, well-born
24   *from a gentleman to a fool.* Julia quibbles on 'de-
        scended', the understood meaning of *derived*.
26   *pities them.* Proteus is probably quibbling on the two
        meanings of *possessions*: 'property' (which Silvia
        despises) and 'possessions by evil spirits' (which
        Silvia pities).
28   *owe* own, possess

29   *out by lease* let to others (thus not under his own control). It has been suggested that Proteus is alluding to Thurio's mental endowments.

35   *peasant* base person

40   *masked.* See note to IV.4.150.

44   *discourse.* The accent is on the second syllable here.

45   *presently* immediately, post-haste

46   *mountain-foot* foothills

49   *peevish* foolish, perverse, wayward

V.3.4   *learned* taught
           brook endure

6   *gentleman* (Sir Eglamour)

8   *Moyses.* This was a common Elizabethan form of the name Moses.
           Valerius. This is the name under which Felismena in *La Diana* goes when disguised as her lover's page.

14   *will not use a woman lawlessly.* See IV.1.71–2.

V.4.1–3   *How use doth breed a habit in a man! ... towns.* Compare the exiled Duke's speech in *As You Like It* (II.1.2–3): 'Hath not old custom made this life more sweet | Than that of painted pomp?'

1   *use* custom
           habit settled practice, custom, usage

2   *shadowy desert* deserted place shaded by trees. Some editors take *desert* to be adjectival; see Collations 2.

3   *brook* endure (but closer to 'like' in the context)

5   *nightingale's complaining notes.* The allusion is to the classical myth that Tereus raped Philomela who was turned into a nightingale which sang with its breast pressed against a thorn when Tereus's mistreatment was remembered.

6	*record* sing like a bird
7	*inhabit* lodge
9	*growing ruinous* brought to ruin
12	*cherish* treat with kindness
	forlorn. The accent is on the first syllable.
	swain. The word is being used here in the pastoral sense of 'lover' rather than 'rustic'.
15	*Have* who have
19	*this service* (rescued her from the outlaws)
20	*respect* regard, heed
21	*him*. Silvia was accompanied by the First Outlaw when Proteus rescued her, the Second and Third Outlaws having gone in pursuit of Sir Eglamour; see V.3.9–14.
23	*meed* reward
24	*boon* gift
31	*approach* amorous advance
37	*tender* precious, dear
43	*still approved* continually confirmed by experience
47–9	*thou didst then rend thy faith . . . perjury*. The idea in these lines is quite clear although exception has often been taken to the strained metaphor in the passage. For the various suggested emendations, see Collations 2.
49	*to love me* in loving me
53–4	*In love, | Who respects friend?* Compare *Much Ado About Nothing* (II.1.160–61): 'Friendship is constant in all other things | Save in the office and affairs of love.'
54	*respects* takes into account. The conflict between love and friendship was a feature of Romance literature and had its most famous Elizabethan expression in John Lyly's *Euphues, The Anatomy of Wit* (1578).
57	*at arms' end* at sword's point
61	*fashion* kind, sort
62	*common* (as opposed to 'unusual', but also carrying the meaning 'base')

67   *Who should be trusted now, when one's right hand.* The F text's reading *Who should be trusted, when ones right hand* is clearly defective in a passage of regular blank verse, and so I have adopted the emendation from F2. For other suggestions see Collations 2.

73   *confounds* ruins. The singular verb form with two singular subjects is common in Shakespeare's grammar.

76   *tender* offer

77   *commit* sin, transgress

78   *receive* acknowledge

83   *All that was mine in Silvia I give thee.* This line has been much discussed, and has been attacked as weak, psychologically implausible, and dramatically impossible. Some defenders of the play have noted that it would have been much more acceptable to Elizabethan audiences as they would have been steeped in the Romance conflicts between love and friendship, and others have suggested that it must be viewed symbolically as a necessary step in the restoration of harmony. One editor argues that it is deliberately ambiguous and Valentine means only that the love he formerly bore for Proteus, which was like the love he currently feels for Silvia, he now gives back to his friend. Julia, however, believes that Valentine is surrendering his mistress to Proteus and so faints. See also An Account of the Text, page 203, and Introduction, pages 38–9. In Thomas Elyot's *The Book of the Governor* (1531), which has been suggested as a possible source for the play, Gisippus tells his friend Titus: 'Here I renounce to you clearly all my title and interest that I now have or might have in that fair maiden' (page 216).

86   *wag* boy

88–96   *O, good sir, my master . . . to Silvia.* Because this passage contradicts the action at IV.4.129–34, and as Silvia is inexplicably silent, many critics have

suspected abridgement at this point; see An Account
of the Text, page 203.

95   *cry you mercy* beg your pardon
98   *depart* departure.
102–10 *Behold her that gave aim to all thy oaths . . . their
        minds.* In *La Diana*, Felix (Proteus) and Felismena
        (Julia) have a final meeting in which Felismena
        strikes a similar note: '"In the habit of a tender
        and dainty lady I loved thee more than thou canst
        imagine; and in the habit of a base page I served
        thee (a thing more contrary to my rest and reputation
        than I mean now to rehearse)"' (*Elizabethan Love
        Stories*, page 156).
102   *gave aim to* was the object of
104   *root* bottom of the heart. The allusion is to the stud
        marking the centre of an archery target (continuing
        the metaphor started by Julia in line 102).
105   *this habit* (her page's clothes)
106   *took* taken
107–8   *if shame live | In a disguise of love* if there be anything
        shameful in a disguise assumed because of love. It is
        possible that Julia is alluding to Proteus's duplicity:
        'if there is any shame in someone who is but a false
        representation of the lover'.
111–16 *Than men their minds? . . . constant eye.* In *La
        Diana*, Felix (Proteus) undergoes a similar rapid
        repentance: 'When the knight heard Felismena's
        words, and knew them all to be as true as he was
        disloyal, his heart by this strange and sudden
        accident recovered some force again to see what
        great injury he had done her' (*Elizabethan Love
        Stories*, page 156).
112   *constant* faithful, loyal
114   *Inconstancy falls off ere it begins* the inconstant man is
        unfaithful before he even begins to love
115–16 *What is in Silvia's face, but I may spy | More fresh in
        Julia's with a constant eye?* In *La Diana* much is made

of the superiority of Felismena's (Julia's) beauty to Celia's (Silvia's).

118   *close* union (with perhaps an allusion to the musical meaning 'a harmonious ending after discord')

127   *give back* retire, back off

128   *measure* the reach (of a sword)

130   *Verona shall not hold thee.* This is the last of the geographical confusions in the play. Thurio is, of course, a citizen of Milan. See An Account of the Text, page 203, and Collations 2.

     hold thee keep you safe. The emendation 'hold me' has been suggested with some plausibility.

132   *I dare thee but to breathe upon my love.* This strikes a different note from Valentine's lines offering Silvia to Proteus, and perhaps provides some support for the suggestion of deliberate ambiguity in the line; see note to line 83.

138   *make such means* make such efforts, take such pains

139   *such slight conditions* such easy terms ('conditions' has four syllables here)

142   *worthy of an empress' love.* Compare II.4.74 where the Duke describes Proteus in the same terms. Some editors have taken this to mean that Silvia is the Duke's heir.

144   *repeal* recall

145   *Plead a new state.* The term is from rhetoric, with *state* meaning 'the point in question or debate between contending parties, as it emerges from their pleadings'. The Duke is saying that he takes up a new position (on the question of Valentine's merits).

147   *derived* descended

153   *kept withal* lived with

157   *They are reformèd, civil, full of good.* This is presumably the result of Valentine's restraining influence, but is hardly consistent with what we have heard at lines 14–15.

161   *include* conclude

jars discords, disagreements

162   *triumphs* pageants, public festivities

         solemnity festivity

163   *dare be bold* will presume

166–7   DUKE *I think the boy hath grace in him; he blushes.* |
         VALENTINE *I warrant you, my lord – more grace than
         boy.* The Duke's allusion is to the proverb 'Blushing
         is virtue's colour' (bashfulness is a sign of grace).
         Valentine quibbles on the other meaning of *grace* ('a
         graceful woman').

170   *That* so that

         wonder marvel at

         fortunèd happened

172   *discoverèd* disclosed

173   *our* (Valentine's and Silvia's)

AN ACCOUNT OF THE TEXT

The Two Gentlemen of Verona was first published in the Folio of 1623 in which it is the second play in the volume. A collation of the bulk of the extant copies of the Folio indicates that some pages of the play were subjected to careful proof-reading and correction during the printing, for the details of which see Collations 1. This text is the only one which has any authority; the texts found in the later Folios of 1632, 1664, and 1685 make some obvious corrections but are all ultimately based on the first printing.

The Folio text has certain unusual features shared by only one other play in the volume, *The Merry Wives of Windsor*. First, apart from the endings of the scenes, the marking of characters' exits is notably absent, only four (those at I.1.62; I.2.49; II.1.127; and II.4.189) being signalled. Secondly, all entrances are bunched at the heads of the scenes; for example, the Folio stage direction at the beginning of V.4 reads '*Enter Valentine, Protheus, Siluia, Iulia, Duke, Thurio, Out-lawes.*', although only Valentine enters initially; Proteus, Julia, and Silvia do not enter until line 18, and the Outlaws, the Duke, and Thurio until line 121. These characteristics together with the Folio's lavish use of hyphens and parentheses have been seen to suggest that the text was set up from a manuscript prepared for the press by Ralph Crane, the scrivener of the King's Men's Company, whose copying work possessed these idiosyncrasies, and who also prepared manuscripts of *The Tempest*, *The Merry Wives of Windsor*, and *Measure for Measure* for the printers of the Folio.

While it can be argued with some confidence that the Folio text was set up from a transcript rather than from a playhouse manuscript (which obviously could not have exhibited such features), it is far more difficult to determine with any accuracy what sort of copy was the basis of Crane's work. One theory, developed by J. Dover Wilson, accounts for some though not all of the text's characteristics. Wilson claims that the manuscript was a composite or 'assembled' text made up from the individual actors' 'parts' with the aid of a 'platte' or outline of the action which was hung in the theatre for the company's use and gave the scenes of the play together with the names of the actors, in order of appearance, playing in each one. Attractive as the theory is, however, most scholars have viewed it with some scepticism, noting that the text appears to be noticeably free from the kind of errors one would expect in such a process – for example, the false sequence of speeches or the accidental inclusion of cues in the lines following them.

Because of the shortness of the play (some 2,600 lines), the unsatisfactory nature of certain scenes, and the weakness of parts of the verse, most scholars have been convinced that the Folio text is based ultimately on a shortened version of Shakespeare's original play – adapted perhaps for a small travelling company of players – a practice common at the time and one to which some of Shakespeare's other plays appear to have been subjected.

The pieces of evidence adduced for this truncation are complex in nature but some of the most striking may be given here:

(1) There are passages which seem to be the result of unskilful 'cutting' or need emendation to produce sense; for example, II.4.194–6, III.2.75–81, and V.4.55–8.

(2) Isolated prose passages appear in the middle of verse scenes and, conversely, snippets of verse appear in prose passages; for example V.4.84–98.

(3) There are scenes (for example, II.2 and V.3) which seem to be curtailed. These may be the conclusions of longer scenes, the suppression of which the adapter has attempted to conceal by writing a few lines of prose as an introduction.

(4) Passages occur in which the sense is clear but which are at odds with what has taken place on the stage. For example, at the end of II.4 Proteus in soliloquy says (lines 207–10):

> 'Tis but her picture I have yet beheld,
> And that hath dazzlèd my reason's light;
> But when I look on her perfections,
> There is no reason but I shall be blind.

Yet, this immediately follows his conversation with Valentine and Silvia over a space of seventeen lines (97–113). This contradiction, taken together with the use made of Silvia's portrait at IV.2.117–29 and IV.4.83–4, 112–17, 181–202, may suggest that there was originally a scene preceding II.4 in which Valentine showed Proteus a portrait of Silvia with which he became infatuated.

(5) The time-sequence of the play is confused; for example, some scholars have suggested that a break is necessary at III.1.187 and that an interval is needed between IV.3 and IV.4.

(6) The use of names is sometimes inconsistent; for example, the Duke of Milan is referred to sometimes as a duke and sometimes as an emperor, and Antonio's servant appears on some occasions as 'Panthino' and on others as 'Panthion'.

(7) The location of scenes is not always clear; for example, at II.5.1 Speed, in Milan, welcomes Launce to Padua; at III.1.81 the Duke of Milan speaks of 'a lady in Verona here' (F); and at V.4.130 Valentine addresses Thurio, a Milanese, as if he were a citizen of Verona.

(8) The final scene contains a number of puzzling and unsatisfactory features such as Proteus's unbelievably rapid repentance, Valentine's ready acceptance of it and offer of Silvia to his friend, and Silvia's unnatural silence for some 115 lines.

In conclusion, while there is no general agreement either on the various solutions offered to explain the above difficulties or on the nature of the manuscript which was the source of the Folio text, it is fair to say that most scholars believe that what we have is an imperfect and probably shortened version of Shakespeare's play, but one which was sufficiently close to the original to have persuaded John Heminges and Henry Condell, Shakespeare's fellow-actors and the editors of the Folio, to include it in their collection as the poet's work.

COLLATIONS

The following lists are *selective*. They include the more important and interesting variants. Minor changes which are not disputed, small variations in word order, mislineation, obvious misprints, and grammatical corrections not affecting the sense are not usually included here.

I

Below are listed departures in the present text of *The Two Gentlemen of Verona* from that of the Folio (F), whose readings are given on the right of the square bracket. Most of these alterations were first made by eighteenth-century editors of the play. Some of these departures were made in one of the seventeenth-century reprints of the Folio (F2, F3, and F4) and are so indicated.

I.i.	12	haply] (hap'ly)
	43	dwells,] dwels;
	65	leave] loue
	75	An] And
	77	I a sheep] (F2); I Sheepe
	110–13	PROTEUS But what said she? | *Speed nods* | A nod? | SPEED Ay. | PROTEUS Nod-ay? Why, that's noddy.] *Pro.* But what said she? | *Sp.* I. | *Pro.* Nod-I, why that's noddy.

I.1.	140	What said she? Nothing?] What said she, nothing?
	142	testerned] (F2); cestern'd
I.2.	83	'Light o'love'] *Light O, Loue*
	96	your] (F2); you
I.3.	24	whither] whether
	88	father calls] Fathers call's
II.1.	19	malcontent] Male-content
	93	give] 'giue
	108	Please you command, a] (Please you command) a
II.2.	19	I come] I come, I come
II.3.	26	an old woman] a would-woman
35, 36, 38, 49		tied] tide
	36	tied] Tide
	47	my] thy
II.4.	11	Haply] Hap'ly
	34	madam. We] Madam, we
	59	know] knew
	91	Nay, then,] Nay then
	106	worthy mistress] (F2); worthy a Mistresse
	114	SERVANT] *Thur.*
	155	too] to
	164	makes] make
	172–3	likes	Only for his possessions are so huge,] likes	(Onely . . . huge)
	175	love, thou knowest, is full of jealousy.] Loue (thou know'st is full of iealousie.)
	194	Is it mine eye, or] It is mine, or
II.5.	1	Milan] *Padua*
	37	thou that] (F2); thou that that
	46	wilt, go] wilt goe
II.6.	1, 2	forsworn;] forsworne?
II.7.	37	rest as,] rest, as
		turmoil,] turmoile
	67	withal] (F2); with all
III.1.	81	lady of Verona] Lady in *Verona*

III.1.   173 self – a] selfe. A

271 *Imprimis*] *Inprimis*

278 master's ship] Mastership

291 try] *some copies of* F *have* thy

293 *Imprimis*] Inprimi

313 follow] *some copies of* F *have* followes

315 *be kissed fasting*] be fasting

323 talk] *some copies of* F *have* take

346 last] *some copies of* F *have this word omitted*

III.2.   14 grievously] *some copies of* F *have* heauily

IV.1.   10 he's] he is

33 travel] trauaile

34 been miserable] beene often miserable

49 An heir, and near allied] And heire and Neece, alide

IV.2. 110 his] her

IV.3.   17 abhors] abhor'd

40 Recking] Wreaking

IV.4.   5 precisely, 'Thus] precisely, thus

45 jewel] Iewell

53 hangman boys] Hangmans boyes

67 know thou] know thee

71 to leave] not leaue

186 auburn] *Aburne*

V.2.   7 JULIA] *Prot.*

13 JULIA] *Thu.*

18 your] you

32 saw Sir Eglamour] (F4); saw *Eglamoure*

V.4.   6 distresses] distrestes

26 this I] this? I

67 trusted now, when] (F2); trusted, when

2

The following list records a selection of emendations which have not been adopted in the present edition, but which have either been made with some plausibility in Folios 2, 3, and 4, or been made and conjectured in other editions of the play. To the left of the square brackets are the readings of the present text, and to the right of them the Folio reading when it differs from that of the present text and the suggested emendations.

I.1. 8 with] in

19 my] thy

25 for] but; and

30 fading] *omitted*

48 blasting] blasted

57 To Milan] To Milan!; At Milan

67 Made] Make

99 such store] such a store

103 astray] a stray

107 a] the

110–13 PROTEUS But what said she? | *Speed nods* | A nod? | SPEED Ay. | PROTEUS Nod-ay? Why, that's noddy.] (F: *Pro.* But what said she? | *Sp.* I. *Pro.* Nod-I, why that's noddy.); *Pro.* But what said she? | *Sp.* (*nodding*) Ay. | *Pro.* Nod ay? why, that's noddy; *Pro.* But what said she? | *Speed nods, Proteus looks at Speed in question* | *Sp.* Ay. | *Pro.* Why, that's noddy.

114, 115 say] said

122 orderly] motherly; elderly; elder-like

129 at once] *omitted*

133 Why?] Why,

135 her;] her better;

137 brought your] brought her; brought you her

140 What said she? Nothing?] (F: What said she, nothing?); What, said she nothing?

I.2. 1 now we are] now are we

8 shallow simple] shallow-simple

10 of a knight] our knight

12 Mercatio] Mercutio

15 reigns] feigns

18 am] can

I.2.   19   thus] pass
              on lovely] on a lovely; on this lovely; on a loving
        28   loves] loved
        80   tune] time
        97   bid] bide; did
      121   fearful, hanging] fearful-hanging

I.3.   21   and] nor
        32   in eye] in the eye
        49   To] And
        65   there] there's
        67   Valentinus] Valentino; Valentine
        73   Please you] Please to
        84   resembleth] resembleth well; resembleth right; resembleth soon
        86   sun] light
        91   it answers] (F: it answer's); its answer's

II.1.   22   buried] lost
     28-9   are metamorphosed] are so metamorphosed
        37   you like] you; like
        73   to put on your hose] to put on your shoes; to put on your clothes; beyond your nose; to put spectacles on your nose
     108   Please you command, a] (F: (Please you command) a); Please you command a
     152   there] there's

II.3.   21   I am the dog] I am me
     21-2   O, the dog is me] Ay, the dog is the dog
        26   she] the shoe
              now] more
              an old woman] (F: a would-woman); a wood woman; an ould woman; a wold-woman; a wild woman

II.4.   54   worth] wealth
        80   he] this
        83   cite] 'cite (= incite)
        97   gentleman.] gentleman. *Exit Thurio*

II.4   99 his] this
       113 *Enter a Servant*] *Re-enter Thurio*
       128 Whose] Those
            high imperious] high-imperious
            thoughts] thongs
       135 as I confess] as, I confess,
       137 no such] any
       146 praises] praise
       160 summer-swelling] summer-smelling
       164 worthies] worth as
       194 Is it mine eye, or Valentine's praise] (F: It is
            mine, or *Valentines* praise); Is it mine then, or
            Valentineans praise; Is it mine then or Valen-
            tino's praise; Is it mine eyne, or Valentino's
            praise; Is it mine own, or Valentino's praise; Is
            it her mien, or Valentinus' praise; Is it mine
            eye, or Valentinus' praise; Is it my mind, or
            Valentinus' praise; Is it or mine, or Valentine's
            praise; Is it mine unstaid mind, or Valentine's
            praise
       208 light] sight

II.6.   7 sweet-suggesting] sweet suggestion,
            if thou hast] if I have
        21 thus] this
            by] but
        24 in] to
        37 pretended] intended

II.7.   18 inly] inchly
        24 dammest] damp'st
        32 wild] wide; mild
        70 of infinite] as infinite; of the infinite; o' the
            infinite
        85 longing] loving
        89 to] do

III.1. 21 unprevented] unprepared
        81 lady of Verona] (F: Lady in *Verona*); lady in
            Milan; lady in Milano; lady, sir, in Milan

III.1. 149 *should*] would
        173 self – a] (F: selfe. A); self: ah,; self. Ah!
        185 his] this; is
        240 As] An
             anthem] Amen
        263 one knave] one kind of knave; one kind; one in love
        271 cate-log] catalogue; cat-log
        293 *Imprimis*] (F: Inprimi); *Item*
        313 Here follow her vices] 'Here follow her vices'
        322 sleep] slip
        325 villain] villany
        343 *hair*] hairs
        346 that last] that
        349 be I'll] be; I'll
III.2.   14 grievously] heavily
         19 better] bolder
         21 grace] face
         49 weed] wend; wind; wean; woo
         55 worth] word
         64 Where] When
         76 line] lines
         77 such] strict; love's
             integrity] idolatry
         84 consort] concert
IV.1.   4 sit] sir
         11 wealth] left
         46 awful] lawful
         49 An heir, and near allied] (F: And heire and Neece, alide); An heir, and niece allied
         52 such like] such-like
         63 this] the
         74 crews] crew; cave; caves; cruives
         76 all] shall
IV.2.   5 fair] pure
         25 tune] turn
         72 I tell] I will tell

210

IV.2.	90	even] ever
	113	hers] her
IV.3.	38	placed] caused
IV.4.	5	say precisely, 'Thus] (F: say precisely, thus); say, 'Precisely
	34	Silvia] Julia
	45	jewel] (F: Iewell); Jewel
	52	other squirrel] other, Squirrel
	53	hangman boys] (F: Hangmans boyes); Hangman's boys
	67	know thou] (F: know thee); know that
	71	to leave] (F: not leaue); not love; nor love
	127	new-found] new coined
	152	pinched] pitched; pinced
	179	my] his
	189	grey as glass] green as grass
	198	statue] statued; sainted; statua; shadow
V.2.	17	peace.] peace?
	32	you saw Sir Eglamour] (F: you saw *Eglamoure*); you say you saw Sir Eglamour
V.3.	8	Moyses] Moses
V.4.	2	This shadowy desert] These shadowy, desert
	47	rend thy] rent thy; candy
	49	Descended] Re-rented; Discandied
		perjury,] perjury.
		love] deceive
	57	woo] move
	63	treacherous] though treacherous
	67	trusted now, when one's right] (F: trusted, when ones right); trusted, when one's own right
	71	time most accurst] time most curst; time accurst
	83	mine] thine
		I give] I'd give; I 'give (= forgive)
	114	Inconstancy] In constancy
	130	Verona shall not hold thee] Milan shall not behold thee; Milan shall not hold thee; Milan

        e'en shall not hold thee; Milano shall not hold
        thee; Verona shall not hold me

V.4.   145 Plead] Plant
              state] statute
              unrivalled] arrivalled
     161 include] conclude
     162 rare] all

3

In the Folio text, for the majority of the scenes, the opening
stage direction indicates the entry of all the characters who
appear in the scene at any point, and there is some final indication of clearing the stage. Within the scenes there are no indications of entry of characters at appropriate points, and there are
only four examples of marked exits (at I.1.62; I.2.49; II.1.127;
II.4.189). In the present edition, the stage directions at the
opening of scenes have been corrected and the Folio's exits
have been retained. All other stage directions (entrances and
exits within the scenes and indications of stage action) have
been supplied by the present editor.

4

The following list of characters appears at the end of the text
in the Folio. There is no general agreement about who composed it.

The names of all the Actors.

Duke : Father to Siluia.
Valentine.⎫
Protheus.⎭ *the two Gentlemen.*
Anthonio : father to Protheus.
Thurio : a foolish riuall to Valentine.
Eglamoure : Agent for Siluia in her escape.
Host : where Iulia lodges.
Out-lawes with Valentine.
Speed : a clownish seruant to Valentine.

Launce : the like to Protheus.
Panthion : seruant to Antonio.
Iulia : beloued of Protheus.
Siluia : beloued of Valentine.
Lucetta : waighting-woman to Iulia.

MORE ABOUT PENGUINS

Penguin Book News, which appears every month, contains details of all the new books issued by Penguins as they are published. From time to time it is supplemented by *Penguins in Print*, which is a complete list of all books published by Penguins which are in print. (There are over three thousand of these.)

A specimen copy of *Penguin Book News* will be sent to you free on request, and you can become a subscriber for the price of the postage – 3s for a year's issues (including the complete lists). Just write to Dept EP, Penguin Books Ltd, Harmondsworth, Middlesex, enclosing a cheque or postal order, and your name will be added to the mailing list.

Some books in the Penguin Shakespeare Library are described on the following pages.

Note: *Penguin Book News* and *Penguins in Print* are not available in the U.S.A. or Canada

PENGUIN SHAKESPEARE LIBRARY

GENERAL EDITOR: T. J. B. SPENCER

This new series is being issued at the same time as the New Penguin Shakespeare, also edited by Professor Spencer, and is designed to supplement that edition with critical works, source-books, and other aids to the understanding of Shakespeare.

SHAKESPEARE AND THE IDEA OF THE PLAY

ANNE RIGHTER

What was Shakespeare's attitude towards the theatre? How far did he share contemporary assumptions about the stage, and in what respects was he an experimental dramatist?

In this book Anne Righter discusses Shakespeare's plays in relation to sixteenth-century dramatic ideas and considers how the relationship between actors and audience changed after the medieval plays. Shakespeare's plays are covered chronologically under such topics as the play metaphor and its proliferation into figures of shadows and dreams, the player king, the plot devices of deceit and disguise, and the use of the actor image in the major tragedies. Mrs Righter argues that Shakespeare finally developed a strong revulsion from the theatre which is reflected in the imagery of his last plays.

'I have never before read a book (is there one?) which invited me to consider Shakespeare's achievement from this point of view. The result is one of those extremely rare critical works that change one's attitude towards the subject' – John Wain in the *Observer*

Penguin Shakespeare Library

SHAKESPEARE'S PLUTARCH

EDITED BY T. J. B. SPENCER

'Worthy to stand with Malory's *Morte d'Arthur* on either side the English Bible' – George Wyndham on North's Plutarch (1895).

Shakespeare's use of his sources has always been of absorbing interest, and North's translation of Plutarch's *Parallel Lives* of Greek and Roman heroes is among the most important of these. In this volume an important editorial task has been undertaken by Professor T. J. B. Spencer, Director of the Shakespeare Institute and Professor of English at Birmingham University. Four lives from North's Plutarch – those of Julius Caesar, Brutus, Marcus Antonius, and Coriolanus – have been collated with extracts from the plays for which they were the main sources. In this way the reader can see, almost at a glance, how and why Shakespeare adapted his source.

These colourful biographies must have been a rich reading experience in an age when books were scarce. Plutarch's understanding of character and North's refreshingly vigorous use of the young English language ensure that they are still a joy to read in themselves. And for anyone who has sensed the creative vitality of the great plays, this volume offers a new and exciting opportunity to explore their workmanship.

Two companion volumes in the Penguin Shakespeare Library,
both edited by Laurence Lerner

SHAKESPEARE'S TRAGEDIES

Shakespeare's tragedies have always been fertile acres for comment and criticism. The same dramas which inspired a Keats to write poetry appealed to A. C. Bradley – or to Ernest Jones, the psycho-analyst – as studies of character; and where the New Criticism has been principally interested in language and imagery, other critics in America have seen the plays as superb examples of plot and structure. Most of Aristotle's elements of tragedy have found their backers, and – as the editor points out in his introduction – these varying approaches to Shakespeare are by no means incompatible.

In what *The Times Literary Supplement* described as an 'excellent collection' Laurence Lerner has assembled the best examples of the modern schools of criticism and arranged them according to the plays they deal with. With its 'Suggestions for Further Reading' and the general sections on tragedy, this is a book which will stimulate the serious reader and do much to illuminate Shakespearian drama.

SHAKESPEARE'S COMEDIES

Once again Laurence Lerner has collected together some of the best modern Shakespearian criticism, mostly written in this century, and arranged it to throw light on nine of the comedies. (He excludes the last plays and the so-called problem plays.) A general section on comedy includes passages from Ben Jonson and Meredith.

Excellence, not inaccessibility, has been the criterion for a book which is designed to interest the general reader of Shakespeare as much as the student of literature. The contributors, therefore, run from Shaw, Freud, and Quiller-Couch to Granville-Barker, Middleton Murry, Auden, and Empson, and on to more recent critics such as C. L. Barber, Anne Righter, and Cyrus Hoy.

Penguin Shakespeare Library

ELIZABETHAN LOVE STORIES

EDITED BY T. J. B. SPENCER

The texts of eight love stories known to Shakespeare and used in the plots of his plays

Giletta of Narbona	*All's Well that Ends Well*
Romeo and Julietta	*Romeo and Juliet*
Apolonius and Silla	*Twelfth Night*
Promos and Cassandra	*Measure for Measure*
Felix and Felismena	*The Two Gentlemen of Verona*
Bernardo and Genevra	*Cymbeline*
Giannetto and the Lady of Belmont	*The Merchant of Venice*
Disdemona and the Moorish Captain	*Othello*

Professor Spencer's introduction and explanation of the links between these stories and Shakespeare's plays, together with the glossary and bibliography, make this an ideal volume to assist the reader to make his own study of Shakespeare's methods in constructing his plots.